Why Are School Buses Always Yellow?

For all students like Howard who wonder,
"Why are mountains necessary?"
Never stop wondering, questioning, and
searching for answers.

Why Are School Buses Always Yellow?

Teaching for Inquiry, PreK–5

John Barell

CORWIN PRESS
A SAGE Company
Thousand Oaks, CA 91320

For information:

Corwin Press, Inc.
A SAGE Company
2455 Teller Road
Thousand Oaks, California 91320
E-mail: order@corwinpress.com

SAGE Ltd.
6 Bonhill Street
London EC2A 4PU
United Kingdom

SAGE India Pvt. Ltd.
M-32 Market
Greater Kailash I
New Delhi 110 048 India

SAGE Asia-Pacific Pte. Ltd.
33 Pekin Street #02-01
Far East Square
Singapore 048763

Printed in the United States of America

Library of Congress Cataloging-in-Publication Data

Barell, John.
Why are school buses always yellow? : teaching for inquiry, preK-5 / John Barell.
   p. cm.
Includes bibliographical references and index.
ISBN 978-1-4129-5732-8 (cloth)
ISBN 978-1-4129-5733-5 (pbk.)
  1. Inquiry-based learning. 2. Active learning. I. Title.

LB1027.23.B367 2008
372.13—dc22

2007040316

This book is printed on acid-free paper.

07 08 09 10 11 10 9 8 7 6 5 4 3 2 1

Acquisition Editor:	Stacy Wagner
Managing Editor:	Hudson Perigo
Editorial Assistants:	Cassandra Harris, Lesley Blake
Production Editor:	Appingo Publishing Services
Cover Designer:	Monique Hahn

Table of Contents

Acknowledgments

Noted student of school change, Michael Fullan, has observed that teachers of the future "(individually and collectively) must develop the habits and skills of continuous inquiry and learning" (p. 81).

Earlier in this volume, *Change Forces—Probing the Depths of Educational Reform,* he quotes Pascale asserting that "Inquiry is the engine of vitality and self-renewal."

Certainly all of the teachers I've had the pleasure of working with on this project exemplify Fullan's call for all of us to model wonder, inquiry, and purposeful investigations about our own teaching. They are, indeed, are our educational leaders of tomorrow.

I need to acknowledge the contributions of so many teachers whom you will meet in this volume: Della Reimer, Jesse Mackay, Robin Cayce, Heidi Nyser, Madeleine Colon, Judy Frohman, Liz Debrey, Kelly Guzman, Victoria Paul, Kerry Faber, Laura Karsjens, Margaret Nutz, Michelle Thoemke, Sherezada Acosta, Erin Kelly, Peggy Bumanis, Kim Nordin, and many others whose classrooms I've visited over the past two years.

I also must acknowledge that this book would not exist were it not for several International Baccalaureate PYP Coordinators who invited me to their schools to model, discuss, and develop curriculum units focused on inquiry: Kristi Bostad, Nichole Rens, Jodi Baker, Melissa Anderson-Rossini, and Anna Hodge. Other coordinators who have supported this project include Ann Mock, Mary Kay Deese, and Wanda Sutton.

And were all of these splendid educators within one or two schools they would most likely be blessed with the leadership of two stellar principals committed to fostering inquiry within their schools: Jill Levine and Ronda Borchert. Jill and Ronda have taken the initiative to lead through their own "I wonder . . ." inquiries by structuring their schools for opportunities for teachers to learn from each other and to experiment with many different ways of fostering wonder, inquiry, and purposeful investigations. Both have been so generous with their advice and counsel throughout this great adventure.

Were it not for all of these educators *Yellow Bus* would not exist and to them I extend my deepest thanks for their openness and willingness to share their insights and leadership in creating those safe, secure environments wherein students feel comfortable asking, "Can butterflies walk?"

And to these students we all owe the gratitude for their taking the risk to share their wonderings, speculations, and ponderings.

We are all enriched by these amazing leaders.

My wife, Nancy, has provided loving support and a warm home for a sometimes weary traveler and I'm always delighted she's there to greet me.

And, finally, I especially appreciate the unqualified enthusiasm of Hudson Perigo for her continued support at Corwin Press and desire to share this book with educators.

Corwin Press extends much appreciation to the peer reviewers who contributed their thoughts to the process:

Stephen D. Shepperd
Principal—2001 National
   Distinguished Principal
   for Idaho
Sunnyside Elementary School
Kellogg, Idaho

Robert Losee
Columbus Public Schools

Rebecca S. Compton, Ed D
Professor, Elementary Education
Director, Graduate Reading
   Program
East Central University
Ada, Oklahoma

Alexis Ludewig
Teacher
Northland Pines School District
Eagle River, Wisconsin

Arlene Sandberg
ESL Resource Teacher
Anchorage School District
Anchorage, Alaska

Denise Metiva Hernandez
Educator
Pontchartrain Elementary School
Mandeville, Louisiana

Greg Keith
Middle School Academic
   Coordinator
Memphis City Schools
Memphis, Tennessee

Gail Underwood
Teacher/Math Coach
Grant Elementary School
Columbia Public Schools
Columbia, Missouri

About the Author

John Barell became an explorer at age thirteen when he first read Admiral Richard E. Byrd's book *Little America*. From this story of intrepid adventurers camped out on the Ross Ice Shelf in Antarctica in 1928, Barell developed many questions. He wrote Admiral Byrd who not only answered with four letters, but the Admiral also invited him to visit and urged him to explore Antarctica. Barell sailed to Antarctica on board Admiral Byrd's flagship, *USS Glacier*, and served  as operations officer during Operation DeepFreeze in 1963 and 1964.

Subsequently, Barell became an educator who attempted to explore the many possibilities for educating young people in nontraditional settings in New York City and at Montclair State University (NJ). His published writings reflect an attempt to challenge students and their teachers to take risks by adventuring into complex problematic situations to inquire, solve problems, and think critically. Antarctica, once a dream for a young reader, has become a metaphor for all educational adventuring.

Now professor emeritus at Montclair State University, Barell worked from 2000 to 2006 as a consultant to the American Museum of Natural History in New York City, helping teachers and students become inquisitive about the wonders of Earth and space.

His current research involves taking the issues raised in *Developing More Curious Minds* and asking how we can work to develop communities of inquiry at home, in school, in places of work, and within our democracy.

John Barell's recent publications include *Problem-Based Learning: An Inquiry Approach* (2007), *Quest for Antarctica: A Journey of Wonder and Discovery* (2007, a memoir), *Surviving Erebus: An Antarctic Adventure* (2007, a novel), and *Developing More Curious Minds* (2003). Contact author at: jbarell@nyc.rr.com; www.morecuriousminds.com.

Introduction

Once upon a time a group of third graders came to the American Museum of Natural History here in New York City. I was privileged to be a consultant there at the time and on the day of this visit, I guided these young students through various halls of the museum for them to gaze, wonder, and learn about dinosaurs, butterflies, and creatures of the ocean.

I remember sitting with two such students in front of a large casing within which was a real Tyrannosaurus rex fossil. We examined the sharp teeth, the colors and textures, and the large cavities in the head. At one point a girl asked, "Why doesn't the dinosaur have any eyes?" This led to a discussion of the differences between bone, skin, and soft tissue. We discovered that the hard parts of the body fossilize over time, but not features like eyes and skin.

At the end of our tour, we explored the riches of the new Milstein Hall of Ocean Life where there are eight ecological niches displaying the creatures who live there and the dangers they face.

As we watched a film on the museum's lower level, depicting huge humpback whales, dolphins, stingrays, and other creatures sporting about, the commentary explained how life began in the oceans: "About 3.5 billion years ago the ocean gave rise to the first life on Earth. Today no matter where you live, it shapes and sustains your life and all life around you" (http://www.amnh.org/exhibitions/permanent/ocean/).

Midway through this huge screen film with oceans crashing and whales leaping out of its depths, Angelica crab-crawled over to me and asked lots of questions. After several attempts at clarifying what she meant, Angelica finally asked, "How did life begin for fish?"

I told her that her question was interesting, asked what she thought, and suggested that we explore the answer back in her classroom.

Angelica's question has remained with me for several years because it was so spontaneous, because it grew out of her fascination with the pictures and the commentary and, of course, because it leads toward consideration of how all life begins. I didn't ask her then, but I now wonder what she understood by "3.5 billion years." I assume that for her, as for me, this is a very, very difficult concept to grasp.

"How did life begin for fish?" commences what for me has been a long, exciting and vastly enriching journey of wonder and discovery with all the Angelicas I've been privileged to meet over several years. Angelica and her classmates are embarking on fascinating explorations of our natural world and of human experience and this book contains wonderings and discoveries just as magnificent as Angelica's.

I hope along the way some of these stories about the students and their teachers will lead to your own questions and discoveries.

As the great Tennyson once observed about an aging Ulysses upon his desire for more challenges later in life:

> ". . . all experience is an arch wherethro'
> Gleams that untravell'd world, whose margin fades
> For ever and for ever when I move.
> How dull it is to pause, to make an end,
> To rust unburnished, not to shine in use!"

> . . . Come, my friends,
> 'Tis not too late to seek a newer world.
> Push off, and sitting well in order smite
> The sounding furrows; for my purpose holds
> To sail beyond the sunset, and the baths
> Of all the western stars, until I die . . .(1842)

We are all sailors on the seas of experience searching for those newer worlds that intrigue and transform our very selves.

Welcome.

Inquiry Overview

One afternoon in Peg Murray's third-grade classroom at Bradford Academy in Upper Montclair, New Jersey, I met several students sitting at their desks forming a small group of five. One young boy was named Keevan and he had a question:

"Why are school buses always yellow?"

Well, I sat back and looked at him and his classmates in wonder. Why, indeed, were all school buses painted yellow? I had no idea. Neither did anybody else, but they soon came up with several reasons including favorite colors, ability to see in the buses in the dark, and others.

Keevan's question was part of an inquiry project we were working on, and Peg and I were experimenting with a variety of subjects and approaches to see what kinds of questions her students would ask.

Keevan and his classmates figured out how to find an answer—by calling the director of transportation in the Montclair Public Schools. I'll never forget how he found the answer to his question. Keevan sat in the principal's large, brown leather chair and listened wide-eyed as the official told him the story of how back in the 1930s bus companies figured out that yellow was the best color.

In sharing his new information, Keevan looked up wide-eyed from the large leather chair and reported, "They took a vote. Some people wanted this color and others want a different color, but most wanted yellow." That's how he understood what he was told about tests that led to yellow's being selected for safety reasons.

I tell this story at the beginning of this chapter because Keevan introduced me to the wonder of children's questions—in this case one I'd never thought of. Here was a third grader asking about what we adults, and most school kids, take for granted—the color of their buses. He was curious about a commonly accepted reality and this led to an exciting adventure that brought new knowledge into our little community of inquirers.

Peg Murray and I were learning how to involve students in questioning various aspects of school life, and the questions were not necessarily part of a curricular unit as are later examples.

This event took place about fifteen years ago, but I remember it so vividly because of Keevan's bright-eyed smile sitting there in the principal's chair having found an answer to his question.

Keevan's story illustrates some themes we will encounter during our journey through several schools, meeting other elementary school teachers who encourage their students to ask good questions:

- Kids love to ask questions.
- Sometimes these questions come from what they find strange or fascinating—"All our school buses look alike! Why?"
- They can figure out how to find answers.
- Working with their friends often helps the inquiry process.
- Finding answers to their own questions can be exhilarating!
- Teachers play key roles in initiating, facilitating, and structuring the inquiry process.
- Students in all classes, at all grade levels, and with widely varying interests and abilities can and will ask wonderful questions if we afford them the opportunity.

We will encounter these themes and others as we meet various teachers I've known, teachers whose work illustrates important ideas about how we foster inquiry in the classroom.

Let me say at the outset that I am most interested in how we help students pose significant questions about the content they are studying. There are several inquiry approaches where we the teachers are responsible for asking all or most of the important questions. This is very important because our students learn to ask good questions from us, as well as from their parents and others. We will visit a variety of approaches in Chapter 5 where we lay out a spectrum of control identifying when we the teachers ask most of the questions, when we negotiate these questions with students, and when they can work more or less on their own.

My primary focus in this book, however, will be on challenging students to ask what we call higher-order questions. We in education have spent the past two or three decades learning how to ask students these kinds of questions and realizing that they do make a difference in students' achievement (Redfield & Rousseau, 1981). Now, my interest is on challenging students to assume more responsibility for their own learning.

Let me now introduce you to several teachers I've met since hearing Keevan's question:

KINDERGARTEN

I walked into Della's kindergarten classroom at the George P. Nicholson school in Edmonton, Alberta (Canada) to see excited students sitting on the rug in the front of the room. Some of their parents were outside their little circle because I was there to model asking and responding to good questions.

The topic was dinosaurs and I'd come prepared with some pictures from the American Museum of Natural History in New York City. I showed the kids my pictures—of T. rex and others and then asked what questions they had about dinosaurs.

There was an immediate flurry of questioning from all students:
"How big were dinosaurs?"
"When did they live?"
"How were they different from 'Daddy-long legs'?"

What I didn't hear from the children was what I'd been led to expect—storytelling. In working with kindergarten teachers over the years I'd heard that children this age love to tell stories and if the visiting fireman asks if they have any questions, Sally will tell about her visit to the firehouse to see the red truck and the black and white dog sitting on top.

But in Edmonton, Della had done something different since early in September:

She had modeled asking good questions.

She had used key words like "I wonder why" to encourage her children to think of what they wanted to know more about. So by the time I arrived in May, her students knew how to ask good questions. Their parents were duly impressed with the kinds of questions they posed, I'm sure.

This episode also illustrates the power of good objects and pictures to excite students' imaginations. I had lots of pictures of dinosaurs, strange, wondrous creatures some of which they hadn't seen and, therefore, they were intrigued by the novelty of these pictures. This is a theme we will develop in following chapters—that which fosters curiosity and inquiry is characterized by novelty, complexity, and perplexity for the observer.

Another theme is the obvious one—by observing nature and human interaction, according to one Harvard researcher (Langer, 2007), we become emotionally engaged and this is good for our health.

On a later occasion Della told me that she had been discussing the fact that dinosaurs and people lived at different times. Sadie was bursting to respond to this thought:

Sadie: If dinosaurs died before people came, then it is not possible for the people to watch the dinosaurs die and know what happened. They (people) have to look at their bones to find out about dinosaurs. We don't know for sure what happened to them!

Brennan: How could dinosaurs live before people? If people have to be born, how could they be the first one born if there was no one for them to be born from?

I was amazed at Sadie's reasoning and her realization that all we know about dinosaurs must come from our analysis of found fossils. But I'm not sure I understand Brennan's counter argument. Suffice it to say, Della has educated these kindergartners to respond to each other's ideas with their best thinking.

SECOND GRADE

Just down the hall from Della's classroom was that of Jesse MacKay. She was currently involved in a two-month geography unit comparing Edmonton, Alberta (Canada) with Mexico and Japan. Jesse and her students "had been looking at climate in all three countries, charting it daily and discussing the differences. Each day a different group of students were assigned to 'research' the weather."

In an e-mail Jesse continued:

"In groups of four or five, students' graffitied questions about any of the three countries of study. Each group was assigned a category of either homes, food, occupations, schools, recreation, language or environment to generate their questions about. We looked at the questions they generated and mapped them on the Q-Matrix (a question framework with stems)."

After charting their questions, students used stems from the matrix to design better questions.

Here are two of the questions students spent time thinking about:

Mackenzie: What might happen if the climate in Mexico suddenly changed to a climate like Canada's?

Eric: How do so many people living in one place affect the environment? (In reference to Mexico City)

Jesse told me that these two questions were developed and made more complex by her class.

Mackenzie's original question was, "What would happen if Mexico City turned into an ice cube?" After sharing this version of the question with the class, (amid giggles that said, "Oh we're just being silly"), I asked them how that would happen and they said that the weather would change. I asked them if they could think of another way to ask the question to help make it clearer and it was revised to what you see on the previous page. This is also interesting because the origin of this question was play.

What is interesting to me is that as a class, they seemed to construct their knowledge in a way that identified the different ways people meet their needs, their homes, food, occupations, schools, and recreation as dependent on the environment, although I'm not sure that was ever actually articulated aloud.

Jesse and her students spent time trying to find answers to these and other questions:

Some students believed they could answer the questions other students had written and there was some debate over the validity of the answers. (We had been working during the last few weeks under the guiding question "How do you know that? What is your evidence?"—which I'm sure is also from your book [Barell, 2003.]) We talked about how we might find answers to the questions and the problem arose . . . what if we can't find evidence? Are our hypotheses enough? (Edmonton Public Schools, 2005)[1]

During this discussion we used the sentence stems you suggested:
I agree with _____ and would like to add
and
I disagree with _____ because . . . (M. Lipman, personal communication, 1985)

During their research they discovered that the reading levels of most information on the Internet was beyond their ability to comprehend and this presented another problem for Jesse and her colleagues.

Jesse and I first started corresponding about this unit because during my visit her question was, "How do we help students develop deeper, more philosophic questions?" She subsequently answered her own question:

In the case of the first question [Mackenzie's], the students assured me that it was a group effort and that the question followed a conversation the group had during the activity.

---

[1] © Reproduced with permission from Edmonton Public Schools.

REFLECTIVE PAUSE

What themes and key ideas do you see in Jesse's unit? Here are a number of other themes we might think about:

- Students can ask quite complex, interesting and challenging questions about their studies at an early age—e.g., comparison/ contrast and projecting possible consequences. Given time, teacher support and guidance (and working collaboratively) they can ask better questions.
- Good questions often come from analyzing data/information, in this case studies of temperature differences in three countries. These temperatures must have shown some wide disparities, for example, between Edmonton and Mexico City. These disparities developmental psychologists (Copple, Sigel, & Saunders, 1984) call "discrepancies," an experience that conflicts with our expectations. "It's freezing up here in Canada; why isn't the same down in Mexico?"
- Students can relate their own questions to a framework of possible questions for purposes of revision, extension, and elaboration.
- Students of this age know when a question is "silly" and can develop it further.
- Sometimes the best questions come from having fun, playing with the stuff we're learning, what Einstein called a "combinatory play with ideas." I think we see just that in Mackenzie's question.
- Second graders can stay with a subject for two months if sufficiently interested in it. Note that this unit included Edmonton, their home town.
- Young children are capable of reflecting on their own experiences to determine where their questions came from.

I continue to be impressed with Jesse's second graders and what they teach us about the potential of asking good, content related questions at this age.

THIRD AND FOURTH GRADE

Community Elementary School #11 in New York City is north of where I live, in Manhattan, and you get there by taking a #6 subway up past Yankee Stadium, get off at 172nd Street and take an Eleven Bus up a long hill. There Robin Anderson, the science coordinator, introduced me to two splendid teachers, Heidi Nyser and Madeleine Colon.

Madeleine is an amateur astronomy enthusiast having received a small telescope from her parents for graduation from City University not too many years previous. She told me of how she gave students opportunities to view the planets, and when I visited her classroom and told her students I was from the American Museum of Natural History and Hayden Planetarium, they

> "Can a planet ever spin out of the solar system?"

had all sorts of questions about the sun ("How close could you get to it?") and the planets.

I was amazed at the sophistication of some of her students' questions, especially about spinning out of the solar system, a concept I'd never entertained. The planets are fixed in their elliptical orbits and that's the way nature is! Period![2]

Madeleine had already introduced her inquiry unit by showing kids a lot of pictures of the planets, galaxies, and various kinds of novae (gaseous clouds, remnants of super massive stars, where new stars are born). From these pictures her students developed two composition pages of questions they then organized (classifying, prioritizing, and managing) in preparation for their research. They were most fortunate in being able to visit and tour the Hayden Planetarium to answer some of these questions and raise several more.

Heidi was also going to develop a unit on astronomy and in our discussions they decided that it would be a good idea of Madeleine's fourth graders visited the third grade to model for their younger schoolmates what they were doing, the kinds of questions they were asking and what they planned to do at the Planetarium during their visit.

Heidi's students eventually developed their own questions during a literature and science unit. Heidi used the content of astronomy to encourage students' writing as well as their searching for information on the Internet.

One of the important elements of Heidi's unit was the way she integrated lessons on language arts into students long-term investigations: "During the next several weeks students learned how to use multiple sources of nonfiction that can be found within and outside the classroom. Mini-lessons included the difference between fact and opinion, how to paraphrase and summarize, using context to determine the meaning of unknown words and how to avoid plagiarism."

What has amazed me about Heidi's literature/science unit is how she integrated lessons on fact/opinion and the nature of plagiarism for her third graders. I've worked with high school students who think it's perfectly

---

[2] Interestingly, that month the director of the Hayden Planetarium, Dr. Neil de Grasse Tyson, considered this very question in an article in *Natural History* (Fall, 2005).

fine to download information word-for-word from the Internet and just provide their own introduction and conclusion. Heidi is introducing them very early to the need for using their own words. (Subsequently, I've learned that New York State standards call upon us to introduce students to these skills quite early in their schooling.)

As teachers we must learn how to use students' questions effectively within a well organized unit that provides structure, time, and opportunity for students to access information they need in order to draw reasonable conclusions and find answers.

Heidi's and Madeleine's units provide yet more lessons:

- That we can integrate subjects into well-orchestrated units that combine students' questions, research, and finding answers.
- That we can and should introduce students to the ideas of what is valid information within our various sources. We need to learn early on to use critical judgment about whether to believe various assertions whether they be on the Internet, in books, or from adults' speech.

REFLECTIVE PAUSE

What else do you see in Heidi's and Madeleine's units?

It is always important to note what fosters curiosity—in this case, amazing, fascinating, and often very strange pictures that today you can find by visiting www.google.com/images, www.ask.com, and the "Astronomy Picture of the Day Archive" at http://antwrp.gsfc.nasa.gov/apod/archivepix.html (accessed May, 2007).

I can't imagine any students, children, adolescents, and adults not being absolutely awestruck by pictures from our two spectacularly performing Mars Rovers, Spirit and Opportunity. Designed to roam the planet searching for evidence in past or present of water, they have, as of this writing, lasted more than 1,000 days. Please visit the lab at Cornell University to view some very exciting pictures that could arouse students' curiosities not only about this planet, the solar system, and our universe, but also about technology, about NASA, about being a scientist, about our natural world (in contrast to Mars), about working collaboratively on a five-year-long project and about the literature of exploration. Here's their Web site: http://pancam.astro.cornell.edu and an alternative http://marsrovers.jpl.nasa.gov. The Cornell site has the best pictures and the JPL site has games and the like related to Mars exploration.

The student products from both of these stellar teachers were amazing to behold, comprised of posters adorned with photographs, original writings, and personally drawn illustrations.

FIFTH GRADE

Normal Park Museum Magnet School in Chattanooga is an amazing center of learning and inquiry, situated as it is in that great southern city. When I visited I had the pleasure of touring several of the many museums with which Normal Park has very close partnerships.

Students in all grades participate in the inquiry process during nine-week units, each of which culminates in students' projects that are exhibited both in the school and, upon occasion, in the appropriate museum itself.

One of the most amazing projects I've learned about since my visit there is from Robin Cayce's fifth-grade classroom. I'll let her tell the story as described to me via e-mail:

> I teach fifth grade at Normal Park and in our World War II study last year, we did experience great success in questioning strategies. My fifth grade class practiced using inquiry first through use of a mystery bag—it was a huge success (and a simple feat!). The point was to try to get my students to question in such a manner that "yes" or "no" just would not be sufficient. Asking very specific questions, and listening to the questions and answers of their peers, was the first step. We then practiced interviewing each other and developing high-quality interview questions. We even partnered with the other fifth grade class and interviewed one-on-one with another fifth grade student. That led my students to write "The Life Of . . ." stories about their friends and we even brought in some photography to go along with the papers. They had great fun finding out about each other's lives in a deeper way.

These introductory experiences prepared her students to use their questioning abilities within the community, where they interviewed individuals who had been alive during the World War II era.

> Students developed their own interview questions and assumed roles in small interview groups. Those discussions were videotaped and are extremely powerful. The students were photographed with their interviewee and an especially powerful quote was extracted from each interview. During our last exhibit night (May 2005), those photographs were exhibited with the quotes and the videos were played nonstop.

> From the Mystery Bag experience (See Chapter 3) students learned the difference between closed-end and open-ended questions. They practiced with themselves and with other fifth graders and then they

were ready to interview folks in Chattanooga who were alive during the War—some veterans and some not.

Students asked about their life during that time, their family history, what role they had in the war, and what they remembered most. Some of our visitors brought items with them. One tiny, sweet, little grandma-type woman had trained pilots in the Air Force. The children were amazed. She brought photos of herself in her uniform. One lady had gone on to win an Olympic medal for swimming!

Robin continued her story with one of the most thrilling and memorable experiences you will ever encounter in any classroom:

John, by far the most unforgettable experience came from a gentleman who was now, of course, aging and just about deaf but he told his team the horrifying story of being in the middle of combat, narrowly escaping and hiding out in an old barn-type structure where he found a Nazi flag. He brought that battle-scarred flag with him to Normal Park—an original Nazi flag! My class was in Science Lab during his interview and when the students who were working with him were finished, they brought him down to the Lab to show us the flag. He walked in and told his tale and held up that flag and that room went very quiet and very still. The children were fascinated.

> "Tears streamed down my face as I realized history had walked in our Science Lab!"

It's very hard to keep a dry eye upon hearing this heroic story as told to Robin's curious fifth graders. Imagine what it must have felt like to have been in that classroom that day and imagine what an indelible memory those students will have of their community and its participation in one of humankind's greatest struggles against tyranny.

REFLECTIVE PAUSE

What are your observations about Robin's unit? You may have observed the following:

1. Peer questioning and reflection can be very beneficial.

2. Students can research beyond the classroom.

3. The surprises we encounter when students engage in inquiry can be astounding.

4. Students can master asking different kinds and levels of questions.

Robin has presented us with a rather complex model of how to engage students in posing, researching, and reporting on good questions and their answers. What must have been very exciting for Robin and her students was engaging in authentic investigations about real stories within the community.

I'm sure the students sitting in that science lab will never forget seeing that Nazi flag when they study World War II in high school and in college.

"WONDER TALK"

What may not be so evident in these short vignettes is the different settings in which students' curiosities surfaced.

In the kindergarten class described previously, we were sitting on the floor discussing dinosaur bones through pictures. With other early primary children I've followed the same format: sitting on the rug discussing a picture book, perhaps of Antarctic Emperor penguins. Within this setting children express their wonderings in many different forms: by pointing to the picture and beginning to think aloud: "The penguins have different colors on them . . . I wonder why . . . You have hair on your arms [I had my sleeves rolled up] . . . Why? Do you think penguins have fur on their heads?"

Judith Wells Lindfors (1999) has identified other wondering statements children share while engaged in informal discussions, often with parents:

> "There's a part I wanted to ask . . .
>
> I'm trying to figure out . . .
>
> This is what I don't get . . .
>
> I thought it was . . .
>
> I wonder why . . .
>
> Maybe . . . perhaps . . ."(p. 61)

In other words, children (some were three years old in Lindfors' research) expressed their wonderings not by asking what we'd call direct questions such as "Why do penguins walk funny?" but by with less formal language. One anonymous reviewer for this book called such expressions "wonder talk," and I am indebted to her or him for opening my eyes to what was happening right in front of me.

In other instances the teacher had prepared students with warm ups, with "anticipatory sets" or "front loaded" the unit with exciting, stimulating experiences, pictures, and other media to awaken their prior knowledge, spark their interests, challenge them to become engaged, and awaken their curiosities before directly asking, "Now what do you really want to know about penguins . . . indigenous cultures . . . the solar system." This is the more formal approach for eliciting questions and one I am very familiar with in working with children, adolescents, and adults.

Here we have a spectrum of settings:

Formal	*Informal*
Teacher elicits questions	"Wonder talk"
To record for a unit	During informal discussions of books, pictures, and the like

You can imagine all sorts of ways in which we use both kinds of formal and informal settings to stimulate children's curiosities. Sometimes we will commence an inquiry experience by reading a story leading to a more thorough investigation of cultures, science, or literature.

To foster inquiry in general we can use the more informal "wonder talk" approach to engage students' curiosities as we are reading any story. Here we will engage students in thinking productively about the story, not just learning it line-by-line.

As we will note in Chapter 5 when using a very teacher directed approach, something we all do initially, we might foster lots of "wonder talk" in order to create an environment that is invitational to students' wonderings. We will not necessarily answer all of these questions, unless students make a point of letting us know that one or more is very intriguing. These kinds of informal and initial experiences, something we'll practice early in the semester commencing with day one, will build a firm emotional, social and intellectual structure for those units where students questions play a more significant role.

CONCLUSION

I hope this introductory chapter has served to whet your appetite for the thrilling experiences that await our questioning the strange, perplexing, novel that we can find in all subjects we study at all grade levels. Watching students form their questions, struggling to find the appropriate words, alone and with the help of classmates and teachers, is a marvelously enriching sight to behold and to experience. Not all of our journeys of inquiry raise such complex questions as Jesse's students posed, nor will they culminate in the dramatic fashion that Robin describes. But each individual journey will result in students' learning, in participating in their own learning and gaining new information as Keevan did so many years ago.

These classroom stories have raised several questions we will deal with in the subsequent chapters of the book:

1. Why is inquiry important? And why important to start early? (Chapter 2)

2. How do we get started with inquiry if we ourselves are not that familiar with it as an intellectual process taught to youngsters? (Chapter 3)

3. How do we plan for the variety of students' questions? (Chapter 4)

4. How can we structure our units for inquiry—examining the spectrum of teacher control? (Chapter 5)

5. What is the nature of a "good question" and how do we help students ask better, deeper questions? (Chapter 6)

6. How do we know students understand—looking at authentic assessments? (Chapter 7)

7. How do we foster inquiry in art, music, and PE? (Chapter 8)

8. How does inquiry begin at home? (Chapter 9)

9. How can we challenge students with special needs? (Chapter 10)

10. What fosters our professional growth beyond the classroom? (Chapter 11)

These are some of the more important questions we shall deal with in the following chapters.

PRACTICAL OPPORTUNITIES

Each chapter ends with questions and suggestions for further discussion and action on your part.

1. Which of the teachers described in Chapter 1 do you admire and why?

2. What are the factors that facilitate (or inhibit) inquiry in your school? How have you addressed them?

3. What does "inquiry" look and sound like in your classroom? What is your definition of "inquiry-based instruction" and where do you see it implemented? (Good question for your students together are, "How do we know when someone is curious?" and, "What is inquiry/questioning and why is it important in school?" One of Della's students, Molly, responded to the latter by saying, "Questioning is part of learning.")

4. To what degree do your students tell stories and/or ask good questions?

5. Under what circumstances do your students enjoy asking questions and searching for answers? What have you done to facilitate this process?

6. After reading this chapter, what are your important questions about inquiry in schools? How can you go about answering them?

"This Is Better Than Recess!" Why Inquiry Is Important

It may only happen once in my educational career—that a student says after a class, "This is better than recess."

But this is what happened not too long ago while doing a reading lesson in fourth grade at Evergreen Park World Studies Elementary School just outside of Minneapolis. These Title I students had been grouped because, like me, they had reading difficulties. When I was their age, I found it difficult to decode symbols and make the sentences and paragraphs meaningful.

Here were six students in Laurie Smith's class sitting around a half-moon-shaped table and we were reading a book about volcanoes and other land formations. I was asked to model various inquiry strategies with them, and we had fun reading portions of the text, closely examining photographs of volcanoes like Mt. St. Helens and, if I remember correctly, examples of extrusive (not explosive) volcanoes like that on Kilauea in Hawaii.

The students were full of curiosities:

"Why do volcanoes explode?"

"What happens when magma hits water?"

We also had fun exploring various models for exploding volcanoes. These otherwise challenged readers had no difficulty learning about plugged-up chambers and building pressures by analogizing these terrible explosions to shaking a sealed soda bottle and then witnessing the exploding cork.

Now, why do I focus on this one event to undertake a brief discussion of why inquiry is important and to explore some of the findings about its significance?

Not too hard to figure out. These kids were having a lot of fun playing with the ideas about explosions that make Earth so dynamic. And they were readily able to use their own experience to make these extremely powerful and cataclysmic explosions meaningful.

But at a more significant level, I'm reminded of this episode at this point in our discussion because I think it highlights why inquiry is so important.

WHY WE EXPLORE

What leads us to be curious so that we want to venture off and explore, whether it be the frozen polar plateaus of Antarctica, the briny Atlantic deep, or the mysteries of the latest novel from one of our favorite authors?

We know from years of study by psychologists that what invites our inquisitiveness, our curiosity, are phenomena/experiences/places/objects and, perhaps, persons all of which possess certain characteristics.

For example, what do you think all of the following have in common?

- Antarctica—its wildlife, climate, and terrain
- The rings of Saturn
- "Mona Lisa," or any Picasso portrait
- Franklin the turtle living outside his shell (*Franklin in the Dark*)
- Local ponds full of strange objects, colors, and smells
- A talking gecko on television
- Warm temperatures in winter where it's usually cold
- The way penguins walk
- "Where's Papa going with that ax?" said Fern to her mother as they were setting the table for breakfast. (*Charlotte's Web*)
- Graffiti in first graders' bathroom
- A deflated kick-ball during recess

REFLECTIVE PAUSE

Now, what do all of these have in common? What similarities do you find among the elements from the natural world and from literature?

Well, when I selected the items in the list I drew from experiences with young children and chose ones that had one or more of these characteristics:

- Complexity
- Novelty
- Mystery
- Fascination

> "Research suggests that whatever possesses 'novelty, complexity, uncertainty, and conflict' invites curiosity, exploration and investigation." (Berlyne cited in Kasdan, 2004, p. 294)

These are the characteristics that invite exploration resulting from our own curiosity. Research suggests that whatever possesses "novelty, complexity, uncertainty, and conflict" invites curiosity, exploration and investigation. (Berlyne, cited in Kashdan, Rose, & Fincham 2004, p. 294) **Novelty** suggests that the object is new to our experience. If it is **complex**, as with a polluted pond or the story of the runt pig, it has many aspects, elements, and points of entry for us to begin asking questions and investigating. **Uncertainty** means that it is not immediately clear or understood what is happening or about to occur—as with graffiti in a first graders' bathroom. We don't know the causes nor what we might do. And **conflict** suggests opposing forces as in a story, each of which has a problem to be solved—how can Franklin learn to live inside his shell even though he's sure there are creepy, crawly, and mysterious things lurking in the small, dark places of his shell. In literature we have the essence of conflict in every story.

When a child is playing with a good toy, he or she is drawn by the elements of novelty—for example, with a new dollhouse, a toy truck, a video game, or a chemistry set.

Interestingly enough, though, one of the best children's toys ever created is the block. This geometric form has no illustrations, no handles, just a plain shape. Why is this so? Because the child can invest her imagination into this piece of wood and many more and make them into anything she wants—a store, firehouse, home, or entire city.

Caroline Pratt, a New York City teacher at the beginning of the twentieth century, was frustrated with overly formalized instruction and created what we now use as children's building blocks in order to foster exploratory, open-ended, and imaginative play, whether single or cooperative. Some research suggests that such play with blocks positively affects the development of mathematical and spatial relationship skills (http://www.communityplaythings.co.uk/c/ResourcesUK/Articles/Block Essay.htm, accessed May, 2007) and fosters cognitive development. Beyond mathematical development, however, there is strong research that child's play results in what Brian Sutton-Smith (1998) once called "potentiating idiosyncrasy," that is enabling the child to think creatively, imaginatively, and be more in control of life's experiences.

Child's play is that natural process characterized by internal control. We make a block into anything we want to using internal rewards. It is fun in and of itself—and internal reality—we make a block into a fire truck. Thus, child's play is that unique experience wherein we are in control in three different ways, ways not often replicated in our daily lives in schools. If we could introduce more playful learning experiences where students are making their own decisions, where they are transforming objects and experiences into what they want and are doing so for the fun of it, imagine what might transpire!

Now, when we are excited by that which is novel, strange, and complex, we may ask questions. But we do more than that.

In *How We Think* John Dewey (1910), claimed that "the origin of thinking is some perplexity, confusion, or doubt." In other words, a good problem or situation full of doubt, difficulty, and uncertainty to solve generates wonderings and questions. (More of this discussion in the next chapter.) More than that, however, is the fact that if we pursue our inquiry, we have begun the thinking process. We are thinking when we ask the question, discover information, analyze it critically, and frame our answers.

Therefore, it is important to recognize that inquiry is a natural outcome of encountering situations characterized by doubt, difficulty, complexity, novelty, conflict, and mystery. These experiences or objects invite our wondering, our curiosity. We want to ask questions and start exploring in order to figure things out.

In other words, confronting an object or experience full of ambiguity, doubt, and uncertainty initiates our thinking and, perhaps, helps us arrive at reasonable conclusions.

Novelty, conflict, and strangeness are, therefore, good!

Novelty, complexity and perplexity foster the inquiries that lead to our understanding and creating meaningful relationships with our different worlds of experience.

MAKE IT STICK

A recent book by C. Heath and D. Heath (2007) rounds out our brief investigation of what leads us to inquire. In *Made to Stick—Why Some Ideas Survive and Others Die*, the Heaths examine why some ideas stick in memory for a long time and others just die on the vine.

For example, in one colorful example, they speak of how to communicate with the American public that a typical medium-sized box of "butter" popcorn at a movie theater contains thirty-seven grams of saturated fat and that the U.S. Department of Agriculture recommends a daily ration of only twenty such grams.

How do you punch that idea across so that it makes sense, is convincing, and makes people take action? Here's how: Bring out a box of popcorn and say, "A medium-sized 'butter' popcorn at a typical neighborhood movie theater contains more artery-clogging fat than bacon and eggs for breakfast, a Big Mac and fries for lunch, and a steak dinner with all the trimmings—combined!" Headline writers had a ball: "Lights, Action, Cholesterol!" (p. 7)

What makes some ideas stick? The Heaths have found the following criteria:

- Simplicity—Get at the core idea
- Unexpectedness—Planned unexpectedness; surprise
- Concreteness—Images, human actions we can clearly see
- Credibility—Believable sources
- Emotional—Make people feel something
- Stories—Involve our storytelling propensities (pp. 16–18)

Now, we can see how this relates to inquiry and curriculum development. We want to select objects and problematic scenarios that are "sticky," that is they represent the heart of the matter (the core ideas), may violate expectations by being counterintuitive, are concrete and credible and involve us emotionally within some kind of story. We'll have more to say later when we plan a curricular unit.

BENEFITS OF INQUIRY

What are the benefits of inquiry leading from encounters with doubt, difficulty, strangeness, and novelty? Much of the current research focuses on studies done in science education. These studies have demonstrated a range of specific outcomes, including vocabulary knowledge and conceptual understanding (Lloyd, 1988); cognitive achievement, development of process skills and fostering positive attitudes toward science (Shymansky et al., 1983, 1990). Other studies (Haury, 1993) suggest that inquiry-based instruction in science can lead to scientific literacy, vocabulary knowledge, and conceptual understanding, and fostering critical thinking.

In their research on students with learning disabilities, Scruggs, Mastropieri, Bakken, and Brigham (1993, as cited in The National Resource Council, 2000) found significantly higher learning with an inquiry-oriented approach. And in studies with "underrepresented and underserved populations, inquiry-oriented strategies enhanced scientific ways of thinking, talking, and writing for language learners and helped them to acquire English and reasoning skills" (Rosebery, 1992, as cited in The National Research Council, 2000).

Some of these studies, naturally, focused on inquiry with high school students—Lloyd, for example. And others dealt with middle school lab experiences. However, one study that focused specifically on K–6 students in California determined that prolonged use of inquiry-based instructional approaches increased the achievement levels of English language learners (Amaral, Garrison, & Klentschy, 2002). Each unit of study "provides students with rich opportunities to become directly engaged in both science content and science process skill development" (p. 220) through hands-on experiences. Students kept inquiry journals in which they noted observations, questions, and designs for possible experiments to determine results. Instruction was mainly in English but students were allowed to write in Spanish if necessary.

Results in Grades 4 and 6 on the Stanford Achievement Test indicated that "the longer they [limited English proficiency LEP students) were in the program, the higher their scores were in science, writing, reading, and mathematics" (Amaral et al., 2002, p. 213). These findings are in accordance with other studies suggesting the possibility of higher-achievement levels for students in hands-on, inquiry-based programs compared with more textbook-oriented programs.

So, it's not just in science that inquiry-based instruction has recorded significant accomplishments. When we engage students in observing, questioning, testing, and analyzing, it can positively affect their reading, writing, and math abilities as well.

The principal investigators in this study, Amaral, Garrison, and Klentschy et al. (2002) hypothesized why (LEP) language students might have benefited from this kind of program:

1. Science kits and hands-on materials built good context over time. "Through the process of exploration, students have opportunities to discuss and learn about the context for content learning" (p. 236).

2. Students had longer periods to learn from each other in cooperative settings. "Students often hesitate to stop and ask questions of a teacher during a lesson but mostly feel free to ask questions more often of their peers" (p. 237).

3. Positive attitudes toward learning were encouraged as teachers encouraged students to learn by "figuring it out" together.

I'm sure we have all witnessed some of these experiences in our K–6 classrooms. Once when I was working with fourth graders using seashells (scallops) to spark some observations and inquiry, I noticed two students busily speaking in their native language—Somali— noticing various characteristics about the mollusks and, perhaps, sharing a curiosity or two.

The LEP study, thus, presents us with multidimensional results from students' spending time examining objects during a prolonged inquiry-oriented program where they had ample opportunities to speak, write, question, share ideas and hypotheses, test, and figure out results on their own.

How much of this experience would translate to other students and other subjects? Perhaps the time for examining strange, complex, perplexing content; opportunities to question and collaborate and extensive use of Inquiry Journals—all would be appropriate in subjects other than science.

And on a purely affective dimension, "Kyle, et al. (1988) found elementary students liked science significantly more after a year of inquiry-oriented lessons than more classical instruction. This study is of note because all the teachers involved had widespread support from their school district, including extensive inservice training." (Colburn, http://www.csulb.edu/~acolburn/AETS.htm, accessed May, 2007).

OTHER DIMENSIONS OF INQUIRY EFFECTIVENESS

But the importance of inquiry in our classrooms does not only depend on support from such controlled, experimental group studies as those just cited. We should be encouraged by other dimensions of research.

Engaging Important Intellectual Processes

When we are curious, ask questions, and seek to find answers, we, at some point along this journey, begin to think critically. We will find information that we need to analyze, compare/contrast, determine reliability, and draw reasonable conclusions, just as Heidi was doing with here third graders.

As Dewey noted, thinking begins with some doubt, difficulty, or uncertainty that we want to resolve. Consider, for example, the second and third levels of the Three Story Intellect (Figure 3.2), and here we will see exactly what Dewey was referring to.

And what we know from research by Marzano, Pickering, and Pollock (2001) on relating prior knowledge to content and on determining similarities and differences; and by Stepien, Gallagher, and Workman (1992), suggests that problem-based instruction increases students' problem-solving strategies and acquisition of content factual knowledge (primarily with older students).

When we think critically and solve problems, we are more likely to seek deeper understanding than if we merely memorize content (Bransford, Brown, & Cocking 2000, p. 236). Other research (Mayer, 1989) suggests that the most significant result of thinking at Levels II and III is that we gain in understanding and ability to use or apply knowledge to novel situations. Thus, if we are interested in students' being able to transfer and apply new knowledge, students must think critically about it. If we want students to understand the fundamental ideas within our units, we will challenge them with what we used to call these "higher-order thinking processes" at Levels II and III.

I previously cited the study by Amaral et al. (2002) on fostering achievement of English language learners (students with limited English proficiency). More recently, Hill and Flynn (2006) present much of the Marzano research, for example, on finding similarities and differences, as well as on generating hypotheses as being of definite benefit to this population of students.

Thus, when students are pursuing answers to questions, when they are trying to figure out some kind of doubt, difficulty, or uncertainty, they are doing the very kind of in-depth thinking that results in meaningful understanding and the ability to use information in authentic contexts.

Thus, inquiring about our worlds of experience leads to fashioning understanding and meaning.

Taking Control

And now for something a little different . . .

I wonder how many of us enjoy doing our own projects in school or at home. I wonder which we would prefer: (1) being given the assignment to conduct research on the fishing industry in Iceland; or (2) being given a choice of which country to ask a question about related to its commerce and doing our own research.

I also wonder how many of us can remember projects we undertook during our school days, how we felt about them and how much we remember of what we learned? For example, how well I remember in high school building my own version of a Wilson Cloud Chamber, a nifty little device made out of a cookie canister that allowed me to see the effects of alpha particle radiation from a piece of my glow-in-the-dark wrist watch. I chose the topic, conducted the research and, with the help of my friend's father, Dr. Charles R. Williams, built and displayed this product. My point is that those projects over which we have some control are likely to be more meaningful (and memorable!) because we are making many, if not most, of the decisions.

> "When students assume the attitude 'I can make these decisions . . .' they experience more of a sense of agency, being in control of their own lives."

We know that assuming more and more control over our own learning and events in our lives can be very beneficial. Consider the following example:

■ Barbara McCombs (1991), a researcher from Mid-Continent Regional Laboratory in Colorado, has determined that when students assume the attitude "I can make these decisions . . ." they experience more of a sense of agency, being in control of their own lives. When students ask this triad of questions, they are learning to empower themselves: "What is my goal? How will I achieve it? How well am I doing? And, how well did I do and what could I have done differently?"

Setting goals for ourselves by this means of reflective practice taps into students' "inherent motivation to learn" (McCombs, 1991, p. 6). When we encourage students to ask themselves, "What's my problem and how will I solve it?" we are, therefore, encouraging them to be more responsible for their own learning. Such agency—assuming control of one's actions—helps students learn more, better, and with more meaningfulness.

One of my cousins, Nonnie Thompson, remembers her father always asking her when confronting a difficult situation, "So, what do you want to do?" This can be life enhancing, but, of course, it can also be difficult for a young person who wants and/or needs direction.

■ Studies (Sullo, 2007, p. 19) indicate that challenging students to reflect on their behavior, on the relationships between action and consequences, uses "internal control psychology" and can reduce inappropriate behaviors amongst school children. Challenging students to set goals and make choices is, therefore, effective.

■ Ellen Langer (1989), a psychologist from Harvard, has done fascinating work with a concept she calls "mindfulness," being open to new information, having potential for creating new categories, and "awareness of more than one perspective" (p. 62). Her innovative experiments, for example, in nursing homes fostered more decision making by patients with the result that the patients felt "less depressed; more independent and confident and more alert and differentiated in their choices" (p. 86). Thus, having the power of choice is good for one's health. What does this have to do with inquiry? Everything, because from good questions come many opportunities to make choices about how to answer our questions.

Similarly, Langer is now investigating a key element of inquiry instruction—being keen observers of the world (see Chapter 4). When I do workshops with teachers interested in what inquiry looks like in the classroom, we spend a good portion of time with observing what I hope is a fascinating object—something from science or anthropology or a work of art. To do this, we must look very closely at what we see, becoming very conscious of different aspects of the objects, making distinctions, close reading of line, color, shape, design, form, design, and so forth.

> *"More than 30 years of research* has shown that mindfulness is figuratively and literally enlivening. It's the way you feel when you're feeling passionate"* (Lambert, 2006, p. 94).

Now, Langer has learned that such close observation—noticing new things—is good for our health and well-being:

> ". . . the process of actively drawing new distinctions produces that feeling of engagement we all seek. It's much more available than you realize: all you need to do is actually notice new things. *More than 30 years of research* [italics added] has shown that mindfulness is figuratively and literally enlivening. It's the way you feel when you're feeling passionate" (Lambert, 2006, p. 94). Another result is that "you end up with a healthier respect for uncertainty, something we are taught to fear." (p. 94)

Thus, being open to new experiences by encountering the strange, novel, complex, and often mysterious in this world helps keep us mentally alert, and even passionately engaged.

CONCLUSION

It seems apparent from the forgoing that if we engage students with objects, phenomena, experiences, and representations characterized by novelty, mystery, which may involve doubt, difficulty, and some uncertainty that we will be able to foster their curiosity and help them wonder and ask questions. Their questions will lead to investigations that, with our support of time, comfort, and access to resources can lead to most beneficial intellectual, social, and physical rewards.

What we have learned from developmental psychologists (Copple et al., 1984, for example) is that encouraging students to pose and solve problems and to search for alternative solutions is highly motivating, challenging, and effective in fostering intellectual growth. As we shall see in subsequent chapters we want to find within children's experiences and within the curriculum opportunities to engage students in thinking productively and with curiosity about problematic situations that are "incongruous . . . novel and/or surprising" (p. 244).

For example, when children are explaining how they will get to Grandmother's house, how they will walk to the fire house, or how they will prepare a meal or a scrapbook, we can judiciously ask, "What else can you do?" "What's another way?" (Coppie et al., 1984 p. 233).

When we challenge them in these ways, we expand their repertoire of available strategies and, more important, we help them realize there's more than one way to skin a cat, more than one possible solution or way of looking at a problem.

Why is this important?

Such mind-stretching experiences foster intellectual development, emotional well-being, and well-managed classrooms.

PRACTICAL OPPORTUNITIES

1. Find objects within your classroom that are worth investigating because they present one or more of these characteristics: strangeness, novelty, ambiguity, or conflict.

2. Play with these objects yourself to see what fascinates you, what draws you in to ask questions.

3. Start your own Inquiry Journal in which you jot down objects or experiences you find puzzling and fascinating. For example, most recently I've written about drops of water falling into a little pool, wondering what factors affect how high, for how long, and to what distance the ripples spread out. How long does it take for the little pond to become glass-like once again? In the news I've been wondering about why certain movie stars receive so much media attention compared with the war in Iraq (one study noted on a particular day the media devoted fourteen seconds to the war and

three minutes and thirteen seconds on the death of Anna Nicole Smith. Why?)

4. Challenge your students to analyze objects, news stories, and experiences to identify those that they find fascinating. See if they can identify some of these characteristics, and then send them home to bring in something that is strange, perplexing, and inviting of our curiosities.

5. Have students record what they find fascinating/curious in their Inquiry Journals. Periodically reflect to draw some general conclusions.

6. Ask your students, "Why do you think it is important for us to learn how to ask good questions and find answers?" Keep a running list based upon examples they continuously bring to class. Create your own poster: Why asking questions is important for all of us.

"How Do We Start the Inquiry Process?"

MODELING OUR INQUISITIVENESS

We all know men and women we admire and look up to. For years, my model of daring and adventurousness has been Rear Admiral Richard E. Byrd, the first to fly over the South Pole and open exploration of Antarctica by air back in 1928. I've also looked up to my grandfather, Llewellyn Ray Ferguson, because he was the man who always asked me, "Johnny, did you ever wonder?" about various strange phenomena. My mother, Elizabeth Lockwood Ferguson Barell, has always been a model for me of a person with a deep love of the English language and its proper usage. She has a keen mind and is fond of asking, "How do you know?" And my father, Ralph Barell, has become one of my most steadfast models of persistence in the face of seeming adversity with his constant message: "There's no such word as CAN'T," a message delivered many years ago when I was in high school and not exactly interested in hearing it. But it sunk in very deeply.

We all know people whose lives reflect excellence in many qualities. I can think of several right off the bat:

- Physicist Richard Feynman's persistent fascination with different kinds of challenges—nuclear physics, bongo drums, cracking safes, and probing the mysteries of a lost space shuttle.
- Jackie Robinson's demeanor—his ability to remain cool, modest, and focused on baseball while being taunted with outrageous racial slurs.
- Beethoven's passion for his music with approaching and suffocating deafness.

- Oprah Winfrey's ability to interview, listen, and share a stage with celebrities and people with good stories.

I mention these professionals here because they serve as role models and can help us create a classroom wherein we encourage students to ask good questions and search for answers. If we really want students to take the risk of being curious and expressing such to us, we need to first create a climate of acceptance in our classroom, one wherein we lead by sharing our own curiosities and questions about the world and about ourselves.

One of the best ways to create this environment that invites students to raise their hands, ask questions, and seek answers under our supervision is to model our own inquisitiveness. That is, by sharing those experiences, circumstances, objects, and ideas that we find fascinating and lead to our wanting to find answers.

INQUIRY/WONDER JOURNALS

One of the best ways I know of to become more aware of my own inquisitiveness has been to keep my own journals, a task I first undertook when I was about thirteen and became fascinated with Antarctica, with Admiral Byrd, his expeditions, and the animals, geography, geology, and glaciology of this region.

One of my first entries was this: "When I am fifty I hope to have been to the Antarctic." I set this as a goal, searched all different ways of achieving it (as a scientist, naval officer), and sailed to Antarctica (McMurdo Sound on Byrd's flagship, *USS Glacier* [AGB-4] when I was less than half that age. (For this story see Barell, 2007b, *Quest for Antarctica—A Journey of Wonder and Discovery*.)

One of the very first things we can do if we are serious about fostering inquiry in our classrooms is to reflect on our own lives with these questions:

- Who have been my models of inquisitiveness—in my family and elsewhere?
- How did they foster my own inner drive of curiosity to ask questions, investigate the world to find answers?
- Who might have inhibited my own searches for meaning and understanding? How did they do that?
- What have I learned in reflecting on my own personal story?

We can ask these questions quietly as we drive home from school. We can also take some extra time to sit down with a notebook or journal and jot down what we observe in our own history. We can also use an Inquiry Journal to begin our own journey of reflecting on the topics and subjects we find fascinating in our daily lives. Figure 3.1 lists a set of stems we can use for our own Inquiry Journal. These stems can also be used by students when you wish to have them begin to reflect on their lives in and out of school and while working on various units.

Here's one recent journal entry:

"3/1/07   38,000 feet en route LaGuardia to Denver/Edmonton

Flying over snow-covered flat plains divided into v. large squares. But what's intriguing is that this plain is bounded on either side—a width of perhaps 20 miles or so—by low hills all wrinkled up looking at first like folds in the human brain!

1. How did mtns arise on either side?

2. What tectonic forces forced the land plains to buckle on either side?

3. Or was it the case—as it sometimes is with valleys—that they represent effects of erosion—washing away sediments?

4. Now [after a few minutes of flight at 500 mph] another batch with hills all wrinkled up looking so regular.

5. What does this tell us about processes of mtn up-lifting?

6. How like processes of subduction and collisions that form Rockies?

7. Then—all of a sudden—a dark flat patch looking as if a farmer had cleaned off the snow—1/4 x 1/2 mile.

8. Or maybe covered with black tarp that absorbs sun and melted snow! What grows beneath?

Summary: Earth forces continually reflect this as a dynamic planet—unlike Mars that has no mtn ranges—Dead."

Just about anything reflects our fascination with our world:
- Reflections on working in the garden, feeding plants Holly Tone, wondering how to keep up all the plantings, why I felt slightly overwhelmed with the feeding this spring.
- Thinking of publishing this book and wondering about arranging a book signing for *Surviving Erebus—An Antarctic Adventure* (Barell, 2007c) in London not far from where the story's hero once lived in 1839.

Our Own Family Experiences

Searching our own family stories for examples of inquisitiveness can be a good place to begin identifying those persons who have positively affected our becoming inquisitive professionals who are often poking at the world to figure out what's going on, often being restless with the status quo and asking, "What if we did things this way?" and wonder about some of the fascinating mysteries in our natural world.

My grandfather was a scientist who worked for General Foods. He was the inventor/creator of the first dietetic dessert, D-Zerta. He was my model of inquisitiveness—always asking me when I was a little boy, "Johnny, did you ever wonder—?" Why the sun appeared so large on the horizon yet much smaller at its zenith (a word he had already taught me)? How we know that the earth spins on its axis? What happens if we mix this chemical substance with another?

He always made these questioning sessions feel like a game, because, even though there was often a good or right answer, I always had an opportunity to try to figure things out, like why the sun appeared different at various locations in the sky.

My mother modeled a love of language and words. How? By doing the *New York Times* crossword puzzle in ink every week. And she still does it at age ninety-two—but not always the Sunday puzzle, which is the most difficult.

She was the one who always helped me learn and understand grammar. "You wouldn't say, 'It's between you and I' just as you wouldn't say 'It's for I or It's about I' would you?" and then the rules of the objective case use with prepositions made a lot of sense.

She also modeled a good healthy skepticism for me when her dad told the story of how once when she was sixteen years old and living in LeRoy (just outside of Rochester, New York) he asked her to look at all the lovely snow flakes falling to Earth one January day.

"You know, Betty," he said, "the amazing thing about those snowflakes is that each one is unique. You know, like your fingerprint. Every one is different from the other."

"Really!" she must have exclaimed. "How do you know?"

My grandfather used his scientific knowledge to explain his claim.

"Well, I don't believe it," she said.

"What?" he exclaimed in disbelief.

"No. Have you seen all the snowflakes in the world?"

And that probably was the end of the discussion.

Fig 3.1 Inquiry Journal Stems

I noticed/observed/saw/experienced . . . and my thoughts/feelings/questions are . . .

What I am curious about . . .

It says, ". . . ." but I do not yet understand . . .

I saw . . . and what I want to know is . . .

I really wonder why . . .

This reminds me of . . . relates to . . .

What's important here is . . .

What I'm trying to understand/figure out . . .

Maybe . . . Perhaps . . . Might it be that . . .?

The big ideas here are . . .

This makes me feel . . . What I feel is . . .

What if . . .?

What I'm learning about my questioning, thinking, searching for answers . . .

John McPeck has recently defined critical thinking as "a certain skepticism" about what to believe, think, and do. Here is my model of what this definition is all about.

When I told my mother that I thought all grains of sand were unique, she said, "And I don't believe that either. Have you or anybody else seen them all?"

Obviously not.

So, we model our own inquisitiveness perhaps by introducing our own models of people who asked good questions. We can do this by reflecting on these experiences and writing about them in journals.

We can also engage in "real-time" modeling of our own curiosity by bringing in items from the news or objects from our recent travels:

News item: Today the papers are full of stories about the conditions at Walter Reed Hospital's outpatient facilities for returning veterans. Questions: Why did it take reporters from *The Washington Post* to discover these conditions? Why weren't they part of routine inspections and refurbishment by the U.S. Army? (*Washington Post* articles February 18, 2007 and February 19, 2007) How can anybody in charge of hospitals (especially a three-star general!) say, "I don't do barracks inspections at Walter Reed"? How might these stories reflect on planning and execution of the war in Iraq?

Object: I often bring in part of my seashell collection to share with students. My wife, Nancy, and I discovered these shells on the beaches of Long Island many years ago. Now, however, they are nonexistent. Why? I also pass these shells around for close observation and inquiry because they are each different, characterized by amazing symmetry of ridges and soft, pastel colors. How did they grow like this? Where? When? And what are they? (scallop shells).

I have also modeled my own thinking with a short story. Here's the first of Stephen Crane's (1955) "The Open Boat":

"None of them knew the color of the sky."

Who? Where are they? Why didn't/couldn't they know the color of the sky? All you do is look up, right?

What we find fascinating, novel, perplexing, full of doubt, difficulty, and uncertainty will certainly communicate to students that it's fun to be curious, that all we have to do is become close observers of our world around us.

OBSERVE, THINK, AND QUESTION

One of the most important intellectual processes in life is that of observation. Yogi Berra is reputed to have once said, "You can observe a lot by watching." Yes, indeed. Watching with a critical, discerning eye can help us identify some of those situations fraught with doubt, difficulty, complexity, novelty, and perplexity.

Richard Feynman told the story of a friend who was able to name a certain bird in the forest. Feynman couldn't name the bird, but his father had told him that the important thing to do is watch what the bird does.

Science and life in general are propelled by our becoming very keen observers not just of nature but of people in our environment. If we combine our close, critical observations with reflections—associations made from our background knowledge—and with initial wonderings we have this little approach:

Observe: "What do we see, feel, hear, touch, smell?"

Think: "What related thoughts do we have?"

Question: "What questions/curiosities/wonderings come to mind?"

Observation is the keystone of fostering inquisitiveness. In fact, we now know from Harvard researcher Ellen Langer that our powers of making distinctions, of noticing new things "is literally and figuratively enlivening. It's the way you feel when you're feeling passionate" (Lambert, 2007, p. 94).

Good observations, "the process of actively drawing new distinctions," Langer concluded, "produces that feeling of engagement we all seek."

Developmental psychologists have long known the importance of observing, of drawing distinctions for the learning of young children. By "enlarging children's acquaintance with objects, sensations, [and] physical attributes" we "expand children's experiences and provide ideas to think about, to wonder about, to use in creating and solving problems . . . [and we] encourage analytic thinking" (Copple, Sigel, & Saunders, 1984, p. 231).

If we want our students to be intellectually and emotionally engaged and to grow in their abilities to differentiate, compare and contrast and draw on prior learning, therefore, it stands to reason that we would offer them many and varied opportunities to become good, reflective observers, keen watchers, capable distinction makers within all subjects we teach.

REFLECTIONS ON NATURE—THINKING ALOUD

Here are some recent examples of my own observations, ones I've shared with teachers on a number of different occasions. Thinking aloud in front of our students is one of the most powerful ways to model our own inquisitiveness.

Recently, Nancy and I were visiting friends in Palm Beach, Florida, and while out on an early morning walk between the ocean and the inter-coastal waterway, I noticed an object on the ground. It was green with a brownish top, kind of oval in shape, and rather small. I picked it up and felt its shiny surface and wondered what it was and where it came from. It seemed like a small coconut to me and I looked up at the nearest palm tree and there were several others. I wondered if this had fallen from that tree and if so, why?

Would this become one of those brownish, fuzzy coconuts you sometimes see in supermarkets that have all of that milk and coconut substance inside, which we sometimes put on ice cream?

While on the same trip, Nancy and I stayed with friends who had a lovely house with a lanai and pool overlooking a pond on the sixteenth green of the community's golf course. One early morning I sat by the pool and watched as tiny drops of dew fell into the pool from the protective screen above and saw the ripples flowing out from the point of impact. The little pool quickly became smooth as glass again compared with what occurred within the much larger pond beyond when a bird flying overhead dropped something in. I wondered what the factors were that controlled the rate of ripple dissipation:

- Size of the body of water
- Depth
- Composition and surface tension of the water
- Size of the object and height from which it dropped

I wrote all of this down in my journal as I often do when on trips or when I'm at home reflecting.

What I noticed that morning was that after doing lots of writing, lots of wondering and observing of phenomena in nature, several of the causal elements came quickly to mind. What would I do now? I would conduct research on what makes ripples and their propagation in different bodies of water.

Whenever I speak with educators, I urge us all to find time to examine our own thinking, our own questioning, and wondering. I'm not sure this is an easy task for those who don't consider themselves writers, but I cannot overemphasize its importance. What I usually say is something like this: "If we want to create communities of inquiry within our classrooms and schools, we, the adults, must model being curious. We must model our own inquisitiveness by sharing our wonderings, our speculations aloud right in front of our students. This might be a new experience for many of us, but eventually, after reflecting on what makes us curious, we'll become more comfortable saying to students, You know what I wonder about . . . ?"

One good way to begin is to take a little time once or twice a week to jot down the kinds of questions we've been asking during that time. What are they about? What did we do with the questions? Were they idle speculations—sort of like the ripples in a small pool—or were they more serious in their importance for our current jobs?

What do we learn about the kinds of questions we ask? Are they complex questions of causality, about projections in the future, about the nature of objects/experiences? What do we become curious about? Is it mostly about nature, about people in our surroundings, about national politics, community affairs, our own lives? Becoming reflective about our own inquiry processes, our own thinking—critical and creative (however we define those terms) is in my judgment a sine qua non of fostering inquiry with others. We must be able to show our own curiosities, our own searchings for meaning and understanding, our own doubts, difficulties, and perplexities to our students when it is appropriate. We must show that we do not know everything, that we are always questing for new knowledge and deeper understanding about our selves and our worlds.

There's no one way to keep an Inquiry Journal, but Figure 3.1 lists some common stems I've used for many years.

STARTING SMALL

Once we feel comfortable with our own ways of inquiring, we can begin sharing some of our curiosities with our students, by reading from our own journals (especially as a way of encouraging our students to do the same) or by thinking aloud.

Bring in an Object a Week

What ever happened to "Show and Tell"? I sometimes receive quizzical or noncommittal glances from teachers when I ask this question.

Well, we still have kids bringing in stuff from home to share with others.

In one Colorado classroom, I noticed copies of "My New Things" posted on a bulletin board. I asked for a copy and here's what I found inside:

"I got a new watch" (with picture of a watch showing 8:21).
"I got a teen titan necklace that you transform into a bracelet."
"I got a watch from Burger King."

What I wondered with the teachers of this school is to what extent we could use such first-grade presentations as opportunities to invite students' curiosities about these objects. Instead of telling us all about their new objects, could students show them and then ask their classmates to observe, think, and ask questions about them? What would be the benefit of this?

Well, for one we would educate our students to be alert, to listen, and to determine what they'd like to know more about. We would educate the presenters to be comfortable responding to good questions.

Other teachers are working on units that lend themselves to objects for observation and inquiry—like quilts, rocks, pictures of the Parthenon, copies of the Constitution, models of fire trucks, human skeletal bones, and so forth. A teacher once asked, "Would it be appropriate to spend the first two weeks of the year building the environment wherein we invite students to ask good questions?" After hearing some others' ideas, I said quite firmly that the answer was a resounding "Yes." If we want our students to become good observers, sharing their wonderings about objects and experiences with each other and, if appropriate, proceed to search out answers to some of their questions, then we need to help them feel comfortable doing this. We need to model our inquisitiveness; we need to bring in objects to wonder about. We need to share our thoughts and feelings while reading books.

Reading Stories

For example, while reading *Franklin in the Dark* (Bourgeois, 1986), we can do the following:

1. Show the cover of the book where we see a greenish Franklin leaning up against his dark shell with a frown on his face, surrounded by his toys in a room darkened by evening.

2. Share with students our observations and then some of our wonderings about Franklin and his predicament: Why is he outside his shell? Why is it dark? Why is he frowning?

3. Wonder aloud about what this book might be about.

4. As we read help students observe what the illustrations are showing us, e.g., Franklin dragging his shell seeking advice from a duck, a lion a polar bear . . .

5. Continue to wonder, "What do we think will happen next? Why? Why do you think Franklin is doing this?"

6. Perhaps pause as Karen and Mary Ellen did (Barell, 1995) to ask, "If you were Franklin, what would be your problem and how would you solve it?" This presents a different approach—engaging students in thinking creatively through what every story has—a real problem for the characters to solve.

7. When we complete the story, spend some time wondering about the characters and their motivations, how the author solved the problem, what students liked/didn't like. What questions do we now have about the characters, the story, and our own writing of stories? Here is a good opportunity to engage in "wonder talk" as described by Lindfors (see Chapter 1).

These are but a few ways we can create the environment wherein students feel comfortable and eager to wonder, speculate, raise their hands, and share their fascinations.

OTHER INITIATING IDEAS—COOPERATIVE LEARNING

One day in Peg Murray's third-grade classroom, she had her students engage in a cooperative learning experience. Students worked hard on their assignment that might have related to reading *Charlotte's Web* or discovering truths about the solar system.

At the end of the period, Peg asked for student reports. One student, let me call her Diane, stood up to face the class, and offered this:

> "We did a good job and found out that _____. But some of our group didn't do good. Timmy wasn't listening and Jennifer kept talking to somebody else."

As I sat there with one group, I was amazed. Here was a third grader telling all her classmates and her teacher that two of her group members had not done what they were supposed to do. All students sat quietly and nobody laughed. This was serious business and Peg Murray had successfully created an environment where students knew they were to work cooperatively together, listen to each other's ideas, build on those that were helpful, and arrive at a reasonable conclusion for their task.

REFLECTIVE PAUSE

Why do you think it is very important to create the kind of classroom environment where group work thrives, where students can collaborate successfully?

Group work can be very valuable in any classroom especially if we value the following:

- Listening to each other, not just the teacher.
- Realizing that each student has good ideas and we can learn from these ideas.
- Solving problems with lots of different ideas.
- Having respect for others' ideas, especially ones different from our own.
- And what else?

We know from research (Marzano, Pickering, & Pollock, 2001) that cooperative learning has positive effects:

> In general . . . organizing students in cooperative learning groups has a powerful effect on learning, regardless of whether groups compete with one another. (p. 87)

Perhaps this is the case because, citing Johnson and Johnson (p. 85), involving students in cooperative groups tends to create "positive

interdependence . . . face-to-face promotive **interaction** . . . individual and group **accountability** . . . interpersonal and **small group skills** (communication, trust, leadership, decision making and conflict resolution) . . . **group processing** (reflecting on how well the group is functioning and how to function even better . . . emphasis added)." If we want, therefore, to foster a classroom where students become curious and persistent investigators of the mysteries that surround them, then it stands to reason that we will teach them how to listen to and work well with their classmates. We need to learn how to learn from each other.

MYSTERY BAG

I first learned of this way to challenge students to ask good questions from Robin Cayce in Chattanooga. She used it to help students learn to ask good questions. Robin placed a recognizable object in a bag. This object was something you would find around school or at home. Then she challenged students to ask questions about it that could not be answered yes or no. In other words, she wanted what we've called "higher-order" questions, ones you'll find at Levels II and III of the Three Story Intellect (Figure 3.2). The first time I tried it with adults we found it rather difficult to do and Robin was doing it with fifth graders. Another version I learned was to ask questions for which I could answer yes or no in order to figure out what's inside. This probably should be tried first, but as you see, it fosters lots of "Is it a stapler? Is it red?" These questions, however, are the same kind that I learned as a child watching one of the first television shows called "Twenty Questions." Here panelists had to identify an object or person in twenty questions. They often started at very high levels of abstraction. For example, "Is it animal, vegetable or mineral?" Then they could narrow it down from there. Another version is to place mysterious, perplexing, fascinating objects in a bag, have kids withdraw one, and then ask many questions about it.

All of these are good learning experiences that will help us discover varieties of questions.

We ought, depending on age groups, to help students learn the difference between

- questions we can answer with yes or no, questions we can answer by reading what's in a text, for example (Level I);
- questions that require some degree of thinking, of inferring, of reading between the lines (Level II);

- questions that challenge us to go beyond what we know, to speculate, imagine, predict, for example (Level III).

We can use the Three Story Intellect (Figure 3.2) to help students make such distinctions.

My preference is for students to make their own discoveries and create their own categories, but we can surely help them by having this or another framework in mind.

Fig 3.2 Three Story Intellect

LEVEL I GATHERING INFORMATION

Describe	Name
Observe	Recite
Record Data	Recall

LEVEL II PROCESSING INFORMATION [IN ORDER TO UNDERSTAND]

Compare/contrast
Classify
Identify variables
Analyze

- Distinguish cause and effect/fact and opinion
- Pose problems, generate solutions, and solve
- Make decisions
- Infer and draw conclusions
- Hypothesize, experiment, and draw conclusions
- Explain (why) justify decisions/conclusions

LEVEL III APPLYING/USING KNOWLEDGE

Evaluate
Judge
Imagine
Speculate . . . if . . . then
Estimate
Apply a principle
Forecast
Create a product

Source: Illinois Renewal Institute/Skylight Publishing, Inc., 1990

INQUIRY AT THE WINDOWS

One day Phyllis Whitin decided to stake a bird feeder outside the window of her fourth-grade classroom, and that made all the difference (P. Whitin & D. Whitin, 1997). Her students noticed the hummingbirds that came to the feeder and, because they kept Wonder Journals, they made precise observations that led to a whole year's study:

> I saw three or four hummingbirds . . . They took several sips. The hummingbirds were yellow green color with a little gray, basically they chased. If one was at the humming feeder the other bird following would peck the other's body . . . The food is going to be half gone because of one hummingbird. (p. 3)

These observations led analyses of language usage—difference between "green" and "greenish," and about metaphors—it ate "like a shark."

Students also generated questions that guided investigations throughout the year:

- Do birds play tag?
- Where else do birds go?
- What kind of noises do birds make? What do different noises mean?
- What is the movement pattern of birds around the feeders?
- Do some birds travel in groups? (p. 22)

The Whitens describe all of the marvelous ways these fourth graders learned about birds: by making close observations, by collecting verifiable data and drawing conclusions, by creating illustrations, as scientists do, to enhance their understanding and by developing that "healthy skepticism" we all of need to use when working with a lot of information.

This is a marvelous story of how a year-long inquiry can commence with simple, yet fascinating, observations about birds seen outside our windows. The students' inquiries became a major focus of the entire year much as those of sixth graders in Harlem years ago described by Herbert Kohl (1988) in his wonderful book, *36 Children*.

CONCLUSION

We can do a great deal to create an environment that invites students to be curious, to share their wild fascinations and persistent press for answers.

We can model our own fascinations with the natural world, with the characters in books and in the news, and in objects we find around the house. What can be more powerful than our sitting amongst our students saying, "You know, I've noticed that some birds around my bird feeder spend a lot of time flitting from one branch to another before alighting on the feeder itself. Other birds fly in directly from afar to land on the feeder. I'm not sure why they do that . . ."

We need to give students times when they can engage in "wonder talk" about objects we bring in and about characters in stories. During such informal gatherings, we will all ask questions and we might find answers to some, but our primary aim is to become comfortable with each other's wonderings and speculations.

And we should establish the kinds of routines where students listen to and respond to each other. I am often in workshops with adults where they see me waving toward the group, because a teacher is answering a question, responding to something another person said and I'm motioning for them to tell the whole group. "Don't tell me, the teacher, tell your colleagues. I'm not the only person here. Respond to each other." It baffles them at first, but then they get the idea: we ought not to respond only or primarily to the teacher, but to each other. I learned this from Matt Lipman and his "Philosophy for Children" program, an excellent way to challenge students to ask good questions and investigate.

PRACTICAL OPPORTUNITIES

1. Start writing your own Inquiry Journal wherein you reflect on what surprises, amazes, and fascinates you. Learn about the kinds of questions you do and do not ask.

2. Share with students your writings, your objects of fascination, to invite their own questions. Bring in an object/picture/experience and think aloud in front of students, just sharing your observations, your related thoughts and some curiosities. Eventually, we will feel comfortable doing this spontaneously.

3. Invite students from other grades to model good interactive, small group behavior. Or bring in a group to model negative group behaviors and have your students identify what they are not doing well.

4. Create classroom meetings wherein you ask students, "What do we have to do here in order to create a community wherein we all

ask good questions and learn from each other?" Make students stakeholders in their own successes. Post expectations around the room.

5. Find objects at home, at school, in the surrounding environment that might spark students' wonderings as Phyllis Whitin's bird-feeder did, or objects for the day like seashells, rocks, newspaper articles, works of art, and the like.

6. Through modeling your own writing processes, encourage students to write in their own Inquiry/Wonder Journals. For those who do not yet write, we can help them draw pictures of their objects and curiosities. Post these also.

7. Involve parents in students' wonderings with letters/memos sent home describing the importance of observing, thinking, and wondering.

"How Do We Plan for Students' Questions?"

Very often I am asked how we plan for the wide variety of students' questions in advance. A variant on this question is, "How do we conduct inquiry and still meet local and state standards?"

For me this question takes us directly to curriculum planning, a process we must engage in prior to launching our unit if we want it to be as successful as possible. When we think of planning a unit we are, of course, going to identify our major concepts and subtopics; we may identify essential questions as well as specific objectives.

Sometimes I work with teachers who are in the middle of a unit of instruction and they're not really sure what they want students to be able to do by the end of the unit. They haven't determined the most important concepts and how they might assess these at the end of the unit.

For this, we need to spend some time planning the concepts we wish students to think about productively. This is what this chapter is all about—in-depth curriculum planning that will help us plan for students' deep understanding of concepts, ideas, and skills.

Our process will build on the work we have already done to create an environment that invites students to freely raise good questions and seek reasonable answers.

One aspect of this process that might be unique is the creation of problematic scenarios or situations to intrigue students and foster their desire to become involved. In other words, we will think about how to draw on the research in Chapter 2 on what fosters curiosity and exploration, what draws us into a situation so we begin to wonder and think about it. How do we tap into students' desire to think critically and creatively?

A MODEL INITIATING A PROBLEMATIC SCENARIO

Recall what John Dewey (1910) claimed in *How We Think*, that "the origin of thinking is some perplexity, confusion, or doubt" (http://www.ed.uiuc.edu/EPS/PES-yearbook/96_docs/thompson.html, accessed May, 2007). Dewey continues, "A question to be answered, an ambiguity to be resolved, sets up an end and holds the current of ideas to a definite channel." We can take a lead from Dewey's very pragmatic approach to inquiry—finding some situation fraught with doubt, complexity, novelty, fascination, and mystery that invites students' attention.

Think back to *Made to Stick—Why Some Ideas Survive and Others Die* (C. Heath & D. Heath, 2007). One component of "stickiness" is unexpectedness, being counterintuitive, violating our expectations. We are looking for situations within our curriculum unit that will invite inquiry because they are simple, and concrete, relate to our emotions, tell a story, and cause us to sit up and say, "Wait a minute. That's fascinating!" I call these kinds of difficult, challenging situations "problematic scenarios" and here is a model.

In working with educators over the past several years, I have used the following problematic scenario as a model. It comes from Carol Cutrupi's (personal communication, 2000) third-grade classroom in Paramus, New Jersey.

> You are responsible for finding a way (or ways) to stop the destruction of the ocean so that the animal or plant life that you have chosen and researched can remain a part of the ocean community. You must find a way to show that your method of saving the ocean will help not only the species that you have chosen, but will also help to preserve all of the living and non-living things that the species is dependent on, and all of the things that are a part of the ocean community that depend on it (interdependence).

REFLECTIVE PAUSE

What do you like about this problem as a way to initiate average third graders into a long study of the oceans? What aspects do you find particularly helpful? How does Carol's problematic scenario differ from the "usual" way of introducing this kind of unit?

What teachers usually identify is the high level of intellectual challenge present here. Students identify a species they are interested in; determine the extent of endangerment to this species; figure out what the ecological web of interdependencies is and how to help preserve this species for the future.

Let's just pause here to consider what's involved:

1. To make a selection from among all the creatures in the ocean, students must know a fair amount about several of them. They will then compare them with each other and draw a conclusion: "I want to work on the clown fish." As we mentioned in Chapter 2, the process of observing and making distinctions and classifications fosters intellectual development (Copple, Sigel, & Saunders, 1984).

2. Then they need to identify a problem and solve it. This means generating alternative solutions and being able, once again, to make a decision—excellent problem-solving processes.

Another aspect of this problematic scenario that I especially appreciate, and have tried to replicate below, is that there is an authentic assessment built into it. Students know exactly what they must know and demonstrate a clear understanding of. They need to use the criteria of dependence and interdependence in order to decide on a satisfactory solution. Remember that every change we make to an ecosystem has ramifications for so many other species, not merely the one we're focusing on. One change ripples throughout the system like a pebble dropped into a small pond.

Easy for third graders? No, says Carol, but given sufficient time (she might spend eight weeks on this unit because at the time her school had oceans as a year long theme), resources, and support from Carol and her colleagues, this is very doable.

Let me stress one more time that having a direction for our inquiry as Dewey suggested and Carol has illustrated is most important to guide any unit of instruction. See the end of this chapter for more examples.

We have mentioned those characteristics that foster curiosity and exploration (doubt, difficulty, novelty, mystery, and so forth). Let's consider Figure 4.1 for other elements found within these problematic scenarios.

When designing our problematic scenarios, we might use several of these as criteria for our self-assessment.

Now, onto a method for developing such a scenario.

Fig 4.1 Characteristics of Problematic Scenarios

Doubt, difficulty, uncertainty, novelty, and mystery— That which fosters curiosity and invites exploration (Berlyne, as cited in Kashdan, Rose, & Fincham, 2004; Copple et al., 1984; Dewey, 1910).

Complexity—That which possesses many facets, elements, or ways of investigating. As Marzano (2003, p. 150) reminds us, complexity arouses curiosity because we aren't sure of outcomes and there are many facets to explore.

Boundarylessness—That which is open to question, problem solving, and multiple entry points where people with different interests participate—not given to top-down solutions. A term derived from Jack Welch's work with GE (Welch, 2001, p. 186).

Robust—Concepts are significant within the unit and curriculum (e.g., dependence, interdependence, ocean ecologies, and conservation).

Researchable—Information is available from a variety of sources.

Transferability—Concepts may have meaning within other subjects and life contexts.

Fascination—That which captures imagination of our students.

"Stickiness"—That which is simple, concrete, unexpected, credible, emotional, and story-like.

What I will outline next is an approach I have used with teachers, both preservice and experienced, in order to help us plan instruction that is mentally, emotionally, and perhaps physically challenging and that leads to deep and extensive understanding of major concepts. That is always, always our goal—high levels of challenge for all students, not just the average or "gifted and talented" students, but all students.

THE PLANNING WEB

One approach I have worked with for many years as a curriculum development person involves the following steps:

A. Identify the topic for a unit.
B. Create a concept map with this concept/topic in the center and web out all of the associations you can make—this will include some of the following:
    1. Names of related persons; significant dates
    2. Associated ideas/subtopics that reflect different points of view: history, culture, art, science, mathematics, philosophy, literature, and so forth
    3. Historical/causal factors
    4. Current manifestations and related issues
    5. Future projections

Here we are "brainstorming" all possible connections and references without any self-monitoring or evaluating. Whatever we think of goes onto the concept map.

C. Then we begin a selection process. What elements/aspects/factors do we want to challenge our students to think about? These selections will be made on the basis of students' age/grades, intellectual abilities, and interests; the nature of our curriculum goals/objectives; and content/state/local standards.

Thus far, we have mapped out for ourselves, or with colleagues, all possible content—the ideas and concepts we want to teach. This is a most important process because without it we have to think on our feet while confronted with all students' ideas and questions about where we want to go and this reflects a lack of planning. The old saying is, "If you don't know where you're going, any road will take you there." Sometimes this is appropriate, but not usually in our classrooms.

D. Now, we consider one of the most important aspects of inquiry-based instruction: the problematic scenario. A problematic scenario is a situation/experience/object that is **novel, complex, fascinating, intriguing, and somewhat mysterious** such that it will invite students' to pay attention, want to investigate, ask questions about, and seek answers. Anything that invites our attention—a strange-looking rock, a conflict within a community, a sudden burst of light in the heavens—can invite our curiosity. Psychologists sometimes call these "discrepant events," or experiences that jar, startle, or challenge our normal routines, perceptions, and assumptions. (One teacher recently noted such an event when told, "Penguins don't live north of the equator." She had always assumed they did, so she started her own personal investigation.) We'll give several examples next. Be it noted here that any initial problematic scenario can and, in many instances, should form the basis of our final, summative assessment. Students deserve to know what we expect of them.

E. Then we can identify our specific curricular objectives. What is it we want students to be able to do by the end of this unit of inquiry? With which intellectual skills, problem-solving, creating, experimenting, will they engage the significant concepts and ideas within the unit? These might be suggested by our district, state, and national curricular standards as well as by our paying attention to our own students' needs, interests, and abilities.

F. Once we have our objectives, we can map out our strategy. We will plan these kinds of experiences:
    1. Initiating experiences that introduce the unit, tap into prior knowledge, and generate questions/wonderings
    2. Core experiences where we conduct our investigations and think critically about findings
    3. And culminating experiences (including authentic assessments)

G. And, finally, we plan out various assessments, which are formative as well as summative.

Now, I have suggested this series of steps as those we can do on our own and/or with colleagues during planning sessions. What is evident in working with teachers is that we all have various ways of undertaking this process. Some of us do it in our heads prior to a unit; some of us use a format that calls for main concepts, objectives and an instructional sequence including assessments.

Before I began teaching in New York City after serving in the U.S. Navy, I had the good fortune to take a methods course with a principal from Morris High School in the Bronx, a wonderful educator whose name has slipped the boundaries of memory, unfortunately. He guided me in the rigors of lesson planning and, perhaps, unit design.

I have never met any educators in public schools who do not in some fashion engage in a planning process that calls for them to identify significant elements of their major concepts beforehand. Only at Montclair State University when I was working with several colleagues to identify how they challenged students to think (Barell, 1988), did I encounter educators who said, in effect, that they never plan ahead, that they just go in there and start and let the class go where it wants. Ah, such luxuries we all have occasionally, as with reading books and perhaps going on exploratory trips. But most of us need to think about where we want to go in advance. This doesn't mean that we plan all students' questions. What it means is that we map out a framework within which we expect their questions to lie.

A MODEL PLANNING EXPERIENCE—"HOW DOES LIFE BEGIN FOR FISH?"

Grade: 3
Students: Average Abilities
Location—Any school, inner city, suburban, rural, mountain

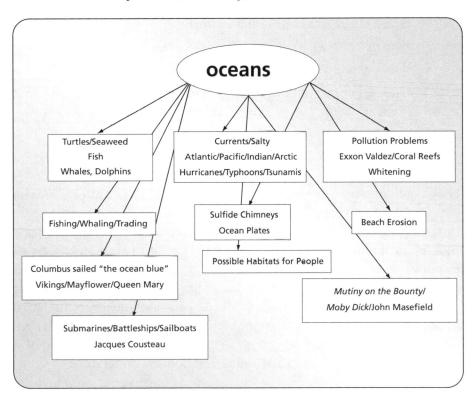

1. Concept: Oceans of the World

2. Map out all possible subtopics/elements:

3. Now think about our third graders and the curriculum: What does the latter call for in terms of thinking about oceans? What do state standards call for? And what are our students most likely to be fascinated by? These criteria will help us select those elements to deal with from the concept webbing.

What would be your selections? Here are some possibilities:

— Sea life and their habitats
— Sea travelers like Columbus and other explorers
— Nature of the sea: salt, currents, storms
— Pollution problems
— Different modes of sea transportation

What might be some major ideas we would consider as part of the major concept of oceans? Perhaps:

1. Humans rely on the oceans for food/transportation.
2. Human activity often changes sea life/pollutes it.
3. Climate change/global warming affects ocean life.
4. Oceans have inspired great literature.
5. Oceans and their currents affect life on Earth.
6. Life originated in the sea.

From this list of potential topics and subtopics, we can now think about a problematic situation that will invite and engage students' interests.

REFLECTIVE PAUSE

Look again at our suggested topics. What possible problems or issues do you see for human beings related to the oceans? And here let us stipulate that by "problem" I refer to any situation that might be complex, fascinating, intriguing, and possibly mysterious. Recall our research suggesting that whatever possesses "novelty, complexity, uncertainty, and conflict" invites curiosity, exploration, and investigation. (Berlyne, as cited in Kashdan et al., 2004, p. 294). As just noted, we can find such novelty in a work of art, a strange-looking rock, a claim that challenges our assumptions (i.e., no penguins north of the equator), a picture of a fossil, or a pond full of weird-looking things floating on its surface.

Here are some possible problematic, intriguing, novel, and inviting situations involving the oceans:

a. Ocean pollution. This is a very big problem in some areas. For example, at the Great Barrier Reef off Australia's northeast coast we have coral whitening as the result of many factors: over fishing, tourists' boats and their gasoline engines, run off of chemicals from nearby farms and global warming.

b. Problems encountered by explorers like Columbus (threat of being lost and falling over the edge of the flat Earth).

c. Devastation from hurricanes (ships lost at sea and damage to land, e.g., Katrina in New Orleans; Wilma in Florida) and tsunamis (in Southeast Asia after an recent earthquake).

d. Creating living quarters on the sea floor to harvest food and study the effects of living beneath the ocean.

e. Helping endangered species survive in the oceans.

How do we frame a problematic scenario? It needs to have these elements:

1. A complex, fascinating, intriguing problem requiring some kinds of actions.

2. Roles for students to play: "You are . . ." a person/team member faced with this challenge.

3. Opportunities to identify their curiosities and search to find answers.

4. Authentic tasks (problem solving, critical thinking, decision making, and reflection) for them to carry out.

5. Suggestions for what to do with their findings as a culminating, summative assessment.

Using these criteria, let us construct a possible scenario that would be intriguing to students:

Let us select the effects of oceans on coastal areas. We have all witnessed the horrible devastation wrought by the Southeast Asia tsunami and by hurricanes Katrina, Rita, Wilma, and many others. I live in an area of Long Island where a hurricane in 1938 cut a new and permanent channel into Shinnecock Bay. So what might be the problematic area/concern we wish to focus on?

1. The extensive loss of life and damage to property, as in New Orleans.

2. The effectiveness and reliability of early warning systems.

3. Communications outlets to warn populations.

4. Knowledge and effectiveness of political leaders in responding to early warnings.

5. Strain on rescue, relief forces—local, state, and federal.

6. Displacement of peoples from devastated areas.

7. Adequacy of relief supplies in the area.

8. Protecting and/or rebuilding seacoast communities.

This list is, of course, too extensive for third graders, but it is worthwhile to map out several options because the more complexities we see within any one problematic scenario, the better prepared we are to help students investigate and draw reasonable conclusions.

For our purposes, let us focus primarily on the extensive loss of life and property. What do we want students to do about this problem?

1. Identify the problem.

2. Gather information.

3. Suggest possible solutions.

4. Select the best, and explain why these are good solutions.

Now, we can think of roles for our students to play. What would be some likely positions of responsibility they might fulfill?

1. Town planners, mayors

2. Ordinary citizens

3. Rescue workers, leaders of Red Cross

4. State officials, senators, congressmen/women, and governors

5. Students like yourselves

So let's imagine a scenario that puts all of these elements together:

You are members of a state appointed governor's advisory board—composed of students, citizens, local town officials, and rescue personnel. Because of damage to other communities similar to yours along the Gulf, Atlantic, or Pacific coasts of America, the governor has asked you to devise a plan to protect the lives and properties of your coastal community. You must study what was helpful to other communities and make recommendations to the governor to help protect your entire community. Keep in mind that these recommendations should be feasible and based on others' past experience.

Now, how do you think third graders would respond to this? We can immediately notice that this could be a very complex process—of questioning, investigating, deciding, and proposing—so complex that high school students could spend months on it. But would third graders be able to become engaged and find some answers, ones that maybe related to having enough supplies on hand (which they didn't have in New

Orleans), having rescue personnel readily available (some trucks full of supplies were blocked from entering New Orleans), and making sure people were evacuated? Could third graders look at the pictures of all those stranded school buses—tires deep in water—and figure out that you needed to have drivers ready just in case, maybe back up drivers?

Could your third graders meet this challenge? Here's what one third grade teacher said: "This is doable with third graders, given sufficient time, resources like good Web sites and the use of graphic organizers."

We can, of course, also imagine what fourth, fifth, and sixth graders might do with such a challenge. Once we have our problematic scenario, we can proceed to those curricular elements far more familiar to all: objectives, strategies, and assessments.

Our objectives might include the following:

a. Enable students to ask good, appropriate questions and conduct research to find answers. (Here our focus is on the inquiry process itself.)

b. Determine elements of community services useful within an emergency and demonstrate understanding of each.

c. Devise a plan to use appropriate resources using other communities as examples of what to do and not to do.

d. Figure out which responsible officials should execute the plan.

e. Understand how important officials relate to each other (e.g., communicate with each other).

f. Present a workable plan and respond to good questions about it (e.g., "What if . . . ?").

Our strategies can include any of the following:

a. **Planning initiating experiences** that include introducing students to the concept of community (perhaps analyzing school and town communities) and engaging with the problematic scenario. Or engaging students with images of ocean storms and how they can devastate a community.

b. Generating questions and organizing them for research.

c. **Developing core learning experiences** wherein we share important new information with students such as lessons on the nature of communities, comparisons of different communities, discussions on important agencies and how they respond in case of emergency (fire, police, hospitals, rescue forces, army/national guard, and so forth). Or lessons on storms, weather patterns, and how they develop and discussions about why Katrina was so devastating for New Orleans and surrounding communities.

    d. Providing time to conduct research, critically analyze information, and make decisions.

    e. Creating a helpful rubric with which to self-assess our final project recommendations.

    f. Sharing your plans with fellow students, perhaps fourth graders.

    g. Revising plans and final presentations.

    h. Planning for **assessments** that should include the final presentations as specified within the problematic scenario; inquiry journals full of assignments, questions, comments, research findings, recommendations, and final reflections.

Now I'd like to mention the idea of "authentic assessment," one clearly articulated by Grant Wiggins. When most of us think of "authentic assessment," we think of tasks that we do in the world beyond schools and perhaps tasks that are intellectually challenging. And this is how Wiggins refers to it, as involving solving problems, applying principles, figuring out what to do and how to do it—all tasks at Levels II and III of the Three Story Intellect (Figure 3.2).

Additionally, Wiggins (1998) suggests that for such assessment to meet the criterion of "authenticity," there must be opportunities for students to practice, rehearse, consult resources, and receive feedback on their ideas (p. 266). This is perfectly reasonable, although not often considered in formal schooling where we take a test, we get a grade, and it goes into the book without opportunity to revise and modify. But in the adult world so often when we have a problem to solve, we get information, devise a set of solutions, and share them with people whom we trust in order to get their input before proceeding to take action.

So too should students have an opportunity to investigate our problem about coastal damage, generate some solutions, put together a plan and, perhaps share the plan with classmates, fourth or fifth graders and adults whose work is related to the problem.

How can we help students obtain feedback on their ideas?

    1. Make initial practice presentations a week before the project is due. Videotape these for students to observe their own performances. During these practice sessions classmates should be encouraged to ask good questions that challenge the ideas presented with "What if . . . ?" inquiries. One test of understanding is the ability to answer this question.

2. With students, design a simple rubric they can use to self-assess their own progress.

3. Read students' Inquiry Journals that record their progress in answering their own questions.

4. Use a response form for students to record what their parents say.

5. Other?

CONCLUSION

We shall, of course, revisit how to assess students' learnings later in Chapter 7. But let me emphasize that it is very important at these early planning stages of units to have a good idea of how we wish students to demonstrate the degree and depth of their understandings before we embark upon our unit.

"Provide incongruous situations, novel and/or surprising items; what is novel, surprising, or incongruous depends on the developmental level and particular experiences of the child" (Copple et al., 1984, p. 244).

All of this planning focuses on our identifying that which leads to inquiry and critical thinking: "Provide incongruous situations, novel and/or surprising items; what is novel, surprising, or incongruous depends on the developmental level and particular experiences of the child" (Copple et al., 1984, p. 244).

Problem solving is a key to expanding children's cognitive abilities. "Giving children problems which are meaningful, important, and challenging is the first consideration. Asking them for their ideas and acknowledging these enhances the children's sense of competence and gives them the opportunity to see how enjoyable it is to generate ideas" (p. 246) and, I might add, questions.

Thus, creating and using problematic scenarios is an important way to engage students' interests as well as develop their intellectual abilities.

SAMPLE PROBLEMATIC SCENARIOS

Grade K–1

You are a space traveler from a distant planet. You are on a mission to explore all living things on the planet Earth. Your assignment is to investigate the characteristics of living beings of your choice and to identify nonliving things you find here. You are to identify the basic needs necessary for growth and survival and compare how these needs are different from those of nonliving things. You will need to learn about living things, their habitats, and basic needs in a cooperatively made book or picture for observation.

Grade 1 (Special Education)

You are a meteorologist looking for a job. NBC wants to hire you but they need proof that you know and understand the water cycle. They need to see written records of your observations. They also need predictions on experiments and results of them, too. Finally, you will receive a $1,000 salary raise if you can draw a diagram of the water cycle and label it.

Grade 2

You are a member of the principal's advisory committee on redesigning the school playground. Examine what we have now: what kinds of play equipment exists on the playground currently. Determine what you think we need. How will you gather information and from whom? Then plan out what would be an ideal playground. Make sketches of your plan. Figure out how you would present this plan to the principal and parents. Be prepared to tell why you think each piece of equipment ought to be in a playground (Ann Marie Pantano and Brian Mackoul, Upper Montclair, New Jersey, as cited in Barell, 1995, p. 28).

Grade 2

Hurricane Katrina destroyed the city of New Orleans. Your town was chosen as a model community to help rebuild. Think about how your town and other towns meet the needs of its citizens. Come up with a plan to rebuild New Orleans as a working community. Your plan will be presented to the town council for approval.

You can

- make a poster;
- make a model;
- make a map;
- make a list;
- make a brochure;
- do a skit.

You should show knowledge of
- what a community is;

- the needs of a community;
- people working together—interdependence. (Kelly Toll Guzman, Denise Poole, and Christine Gill of Joseph Sharp Elementary School, Cherry Hill, New Jersey)

Grade 3

You are responsible for finding a way (or ways) to stop the destruction of the ocean so that the animal or plant life that you have chosen and researched can remain a part of the ocean community. You must find a way to show that your method of saving the ocean will not only help the species that you have chosen, but will also help to preserve all of the living and nonliving things that the species is dependent on, and all of the things that are a part of the ocean community that depend on it—interdependence (Cutrupi, personal communication 2000).

Grades 5/6

"You are an earth scientist who has been hired by a publishing company to create an ABC book on landforms. They are sending you to different places around the world to research and investigate the formation of landforms both continental and oceanic. When you return you design the book to educate future fifth graders about the natural processes of Earth.

You will keep a journal of all of your ideas for each letter of the alphabet. In this journal you will put information you already know, what you are learning along the way and questions that you are still curious about.

By the end of all your experiences you will have enough ideas and have completed all research to create an artistic alphabet book filled with knowledge about the formation of landforms" (Kim Nordin, Rosewood Elementary School, South Carolina, Grade 5).

Kim (personal communication, June, 2007) notes, "We found the students very engaged in this planner [unit] because they knew *from day one what they were to accomplish by the end of the planner.* [Italics added] This gave them focus, drive and excitement. It really allowed for them to be inquirers as they questioned and researched landforms. Also, by allowing them to create their own rubric for the book they felt like they had ownership in their project.

Grades 5/6

For a unit on Culture and Geology of the Appalachian Region, you are a young economist studying various regions of the country. You discover that people in Appalachia live under very difficult economic conditions.

You have a number of questions, among which is Why do people continue to live there if economic conditions are so difficult? How did living conditions become so harsh?

What other questions need you to ask about these living situations as you work toward developing a plan for economic renewal. You must consider several alternatives and support your choices with good reasons and examples from the economic development of other communities (adapted from Barell, 2007a, p. 63).

Grade 6

You are a technologist recently called into a town near the slopes of Mt. St. Helens. Geologists predict that another pyroclastic flow (similar to that of 1980) will occur sometime in the near future. Such a natural disaster jeopardizes the lives of thousands of people. Develop and build a protective device to offset the power of this phenomenon thereby saving the lives and protecting the property of the population.

Variations on the "You are." scenario involve making claims:

> Today's students need to prepare for the institution of a draft—for young men and women of high school age. (I presented this as a problematic scenario to a group of fifth graders studying the U.S. Constitution and there ensued vigorous debate about what they thought they knew about the Constitution, their rights and responsibilities as well as those of the Executive and Legislative Branches. I introduced this by stating that the principal had received a letter from the president stating his new policy.

Suggesting a "What if . . ." scenario

What if the governor of your state says your town and others are becoming too crowded. He is asking you to find a suitable location for a new town and wants to know what kinds of community services we need and why and how you might improve them. (I presented this to second graders studying communities and used it as a formative assessment. What was interesting was that in two different grades students seemed to focus much of their ideas on one service—e.g., police or hospitals.)

PRACTICAL OPPORTUNITIES

1. Select a unit you have already taught and create a problematic scenario for it.

2. Select a unit you will teach in the future and work through the webbing, selecting, and designing problematic scenario process previously identified.

3. Which of your previous units have contained elements that foster curiosity and that challenge students to inquire and think? Consider Figure 4.1.

4. What objects/experiences/persons in your experience have already fostered your and your students' inquisitiveness?

5. Consider variations on the problematic scenario:

   a. Making claims that arouse curiosity—"The oceans can never recover from the damage we've done to them."

   b. Using "What if?" wonderings: "What if everybody in the United States had to have an ID card with a computer chip inside that had information about residence, health, employment, and parking tickets?"

   c. For more such possibilities see *Problem-Based Learning—An Inquiry Approach*, Barell, 2007a.

Developing Units of Instruction

"When Is It Chaos?"

In one fourth-grade classroom, I was sitting amidst students avidly examining seashells I'd distributed for them to observe. These were scallop shells from Long Island beaches and I'd mentioned that years ago there were plenty and now there were hardly any. Hence, we had a discrepancy. What had happened to the shells? I was sharing with students my own fascination and curiosity with this experience. Here is another example of that which fosters curiosity and exploration: novelty, perplexity, doubt, contradiction, and violated expectations (see Chapter 2).

I wanted the students to become good observers and to notice their size, shape, colors, and the distribution of colors and ribbing on the outside of the shells. Here I was modeling how we might get students interested in asking questions as a lead-in to their unit on natural resources.

As the kids began examining the shells, they got excited, so excited and verbal that it seemed as the class would spin out of control. This was amazing to me because not only was their teacher sitting outside our little circle, but there were also four or five other teachers observing as well as the principal himself.

There was lots of noise, lots of crawling around, loud statements about "Look at these colors . . . Is this from the ocean? Yes, all shells are from the ocean . . .What lived inside these things?" and so on.

I mention this episode because the teacher was embarrassed by her students' behavior and all of us in the post-conference comforted her with the view that when you give kids something novel to observe and play with, they are likely to show their enthusiasm in ways we haven't expected. By the way, on two different occasions, she stepped into the circle to help quiet two of her more excited students and focus their attention. And I've previously mentioned the two Somali students at the circle's edge who just kept on quietly observing and sharing questions (head to head) after we started discussing our observations and questions. Some of us are not ready for this kind of "organized chaos" in our classrooms and, frankly, I was at times struggling to regain students' attention.

Thus, not all of us are comfortable with the management challenge of opening our classroom to students' questions and attempting to make them part of our units of instruction. It takes time and comfort with inquiry to adventure into the different approaches that are at our disposal.

MANY WAYS TO SKIN A CAT

There is no one way to initiate a unit once we have engaged in the kind of planning just described in Chapter 4. In another work (Barell, 2007a), I've mentioned three ways of looking at problem-based learning with a focus on inquiry:

| *Teacher Directed* | *Teacher-Student Negotiated* | *Independent Student Investigations* |

This triad of approaches has been otherwise characterized as Structured Inquiry, Guided Inquiry, and Independent Study a term akin to Independent Student Investigations.

What my own characterization has at its base is the concept of control. That is to ask, Who controls the decision-making processes during instruction? This question boils down to asking, Who makes decisions about the following:

- Content
- Curricular goals and objectives
- Strategies
- Resources
- Means of feedback and assessment
- Scoring/assessment criteria

As you might imagine, up on the left side of our continuum, teachers make almost all decisions. Toward the middle, we might negotiate with students on some decisions and on the far right side of this spectrum students make most of the decisions and work collaboratively with each other or alone on independent-study projects.

In Teacher Directed inquiry, we ask the questions and might generate several students' questions and deal with them as we can.

In Teacher-Student Negotiated inquiry, we work to generate students' questions and these become a major element of our content (together with teachers' questions)—we provide resources with which students can answer their own questions.

During Independent Study students are selecting their own questions, with our approval and support, and working collaboratively (or alone) to seek out answers and share findings.

REFLECTIVE PAUSE

What determines which approach you might undertake? What do you consider the key variables that would affect your decision?
Here are some that come to mind:

1. Teachers' experience with various units and with teaching itself. We might be much more highly structured with units we have little experience with and at the beginning of our teaching careers for a variety of reasons.

2. Students' levels of maturity, their ability to work collaboratively, and their experience in conducting research. See Chapter 3.

3. Nature of the unit. It may be there are units that need to be guided more by our questions and our goals than others. Perhaps those that deal with core content concepts that students need to grasp in depth before we can proceed with other units in the subject (e.g., nature of the human cell; nature of revolution; writing stories of our own).

4. Our psychological comfort levels with students' asking questions we might not know the answer to; our feelings of self-assurance in managing a more open-ended approach where we respond to and include some of students' questions in our long-range plans.

   Inquiry is more often than not dependent on our own tolerance of ambiguity, more open-ended investigations and with questions to which we do not know the answer. If we need to know the answers to all questions before a unit commences, we will not embark on the kinds of experiences described below. For some of us this transformation takes a long time. Thus, inquiry-based instruction is not a matter of obtaining new resource materials and changing strategies. These are important but of greater importance is our becoming internally, emotionally comfortable with change, ambiguity, novelty and more open kinds of structures.

5. Other criteria you can think of.

A TEACHER DIRECTED UNIT—OCEANS

Let us continue our thinking about the oceans unit commenced in Chapter 4 and illustrate how it might proceed with teachers making almost all of the decisions. We might opt for this approach because we've never taught the unit before and we aren't really comfortable with managing what we expect will be a wide variety of questions. We also aren't too sure of ourselves in knowing how to help students move from very basic kinds of questions to ones that Jesse Mackay (see Chapter 1) called "deeper and more philosophic."

To review, here are our concepts and major objectives for the unit:

Central Concept: Oceans of the World

Contributing Ideas: Animal and plant life; ocean forces; coastal communities . . .

Essential Questions: How oceans work—move, stay healthy, circulate?
What lives in the oceans and how do they survive?
How oceans affect life on Earth?
How communities do/do not prepare for ocean events?
How to ask good questions about nature and find reasonable answers?

Objectives:

1. Describe how sea life survives in ocean environments.

2. Compare/contrast different kinds of ocean currents/storms.

3. Identify/analyze and evaluate various ways oceans affect human life—positively/negatively.

4. Figure out how to help local communities protect themselves against ocean disasters (e.g., hurricanes, tsunamis, typhoons, ocean pollution).

5. Be able to generate and answer good questions about the nature of oceans/currents and their effects on humanity.

   (This objective will be more important during the Teacher-Student Negotiated unit described next.)

Getting Started—Films on Coral Reefs

What would we do to get students interested in such a unit, to start the process of inquiry, investigations, and learning? Before responding to this question, let us return to Chapter 2 and to what we know about curiosity and how to stimulate it. Recall our identifying various elements that foster exploration: novelty, complexity, perplexity, doubt, and difficulty.

In *Made to Stick—Why Some Ideas Survive and Others Die,* Chip and Dan Heath (2007) discuss the elements of unexpectedness and concreteness as contributing factors. For example, curiosity comes from gaps in our knowledge. But what if there's not much knowledge there to begin with? you have to fill in enough knowledge to make the abyss into a gap. (pp. 90–91).

Educators call this "abyss" a lack of prior knowledge. What can we do? "The way to get people to care is to provide a context . . . The idea is that to engage students in a new topic you should start by highlighting some things they already know" (p. 92).

We can do this with pictures, slides, newspaper articles, artifacts, just about anything. For example, when Cheryl Hopper set about to use the KWHLAQ inquiry strategy for a unit on Africa (Barell, 2003, 2007a), she spent two days showing her ninth graders slides of all aspects of African culture—its wide diversity—as well as the many and varied land formations (deserts, forests, open plains, and mountain areas). Then she proceeded to tap into what they thought they knew ("What do we think we already know about Africa?" see Figure 5.1).

What we are doing is providing a context for learning as well as helping students to identify what they think they already know about the continent. We can start in a number of different ways, but one that resonates with me is, before introducing our problematic scenario, provide students with a lot of visual information about the oceans.

We might commence with a spectacular video from the American Museum of Natural History on "Coral Reefs." This video, premiered as an Imax film at the Museum, comes with marvelous music by Crosby, Stills, Nash, and Young and would be an outstanding introduction to a problematic scenario on what is happening to the oceans.

Anything will do that introduces the topic of oceans, has excellent pictures of oceans, ocean life, various habitats, and some of what is occurring to the oceans.

Of course, if you live near an outstanding resource like the American Museum of Natural History, you could commence the unit with a visit to the Milstein Hall of Ocean Life. (You could also culminate your unit with such a visit.) If you are unable to visit a local museum, you could visit this excellent resource online at http://www.amnh.org/exhibitions/permanent/ocean/?src=e_h. Here you can visit the several different ecosystems, from polar regions and estuaries, to the depths of the ocean bottom.

You could also bring in objects from the oceans such as shells, replicas of fish, and pictures of devastated seaside communities and engage in the process described in Chapter 3—observe, think, and question. I've used seashells, volcanic rocks, and pictures of cultural objects and of dinosaur fossils. Anything will do to foster students' engagement and get them interested in a subject or problematic situation.

The follow-up to such an experience can include discussing what kids saw, what they liked, what fascinated and surprised them, and, of course, what they were curious about.

Students' Questions

While looking at a video and pictures of the oceans, visiting a museum, or taking a short field trip to the seaside, students will do a lot of observing and seeing a lot of new objects—shells, fish, mollusks, coral reefs, and the effects of pollution and ocean damage.

They will naturally have questions and we should provide time and opportunity for them to share their thoughts and their wonderings. A discussion after viewing a video would be a very good opportunity for students to share what they saw and were intrigued by.

They will want to know the following:

- What are coral reefs? Why are they white? How do we help them?
- How deep are oceans?
- How many oceans are there?
- How many different kinds of fish are there?
- What kinds of fish can we eat?
- What causes a hurricane? Why do they exist?

The questions students ask here can and should be accepted, recorded, and posted around the room. Why? Because we can find ways to answer some or all of them as we work through the unit.

What we aren't going to do at this point is channel some of these questions into our objectives, giving students opportunities to classify, sort, and create a priority list that we will vigorously research. But we might get some practice here in asking our students to identify what they think are "good questions." If they can begin to identify such, we can post those on separate flip chart papers for continuous reference (see Chapter 6).

But these questions can help us become comfortable with a wide variety of students' curiosities. By keeping them around the room, we will be able to answer many of them as we encounter new information about oceans and their effects on local seaside communities. We can also, obviously, encourage students to find their own answers and give them opportunity to share what they've found.

Problematic Scenario

Here again is our problematic scenario:

> "You are members of a state appointed governor's advisory board—composed of students, citizens, local town officials, and rescue personnel. Because of damage to other communities similar to yours along the Gulf, Atlantic, or Pacific coasts of America, the governor has asked you to devise a plan to protect the lives and properties of your coastal community. You must study what was helpful to other communities and make recommendations to the governor to help protect your entire community. Keep in mind that these recommendations should be feasible and based on others' past experience."

We share this with students and invite their participation by asking them these kinds of questions:

1. "What does this situation mean to you? What is the governor asking you to do?"

2. "What questions do we need to ask in order to understand what we are supposed to do?" (Here we begin challenging our students to think as young professionals seeking to understand a fascinating situation/phenomenon.)

3. "How can we figure out what to do?"

With these questions and answers, we can then begin to work through our instructional plan. Note that we should have already considered most students' questions during the planning process outlined in Chapter 4. We need not be surprised by what intrigues our students if we've sufficiently laid out our plan.

Core Learning Experiences

Here we have already (see Chapter 4) planned out our sequence of instruction. It may include several of the following elements:

1. Working with several different resources to help us meet our objectives.

2. Including resources such as books, more videos/DVDs, access to Web sites like Milstein Hall of Ocean Life at AMNH: http://www.amnh.org/exhibitions/permanent/ocean/?src=e_h. Searching

with students for other sites about ocean life and the effects of hurricanes.

3. Teaching directly those concepts we deem important: content: nature of oceans/currents/storms and the like; process: how to analyze information found in various sources—the differences between fact and value judgments; how to evaluate Web resources, draw reasonable conclusions, ask better questions, and avoid plagiarism (Heidi Nyser, Grade 3, New York City and the New York State/City Standards).

4. Locating communities like those that suffered along the Gulf Coast from Katrina and Rita, communities in other coastal states, and in Southeast Asia.

5. Talking with local emergency preparedness personnel about how to get ready for a possible storm.

6. Writing in your Inquiry Journal about what you are learning such as new questions and answers to others.

7. Taking time to plan your solution to the problem.

8. Taking time to share initial ideas to get feedback.

Culminating Projects

The beauty of having a clearly defined problematic scenario is that it presents us with a goal toward which to work. If we've used some of the learning activities just described, we will be ready to have students present their final projects to those who might be interested listeners (e.g., fourth/fifth graders, local emergency preparedness personnel, and parents).

We will consider a variety of ways for students to share their findings—written and oral reports, videos, panel discussions, posters, dramatizations, diaries, and the like.

We will, of course, have other means of assessing the depth and quality of students' understandings including the following:

1. Reading their Inquiry Journals.

2. Accompanying their final project with one or two paragraphs explaining how they came up with their ideas.

3. Including other writing experiences related to other key ideas (e.g., kinds of sea life and the environments in which they live).

4. Including other means you can think of (e.g., quizzes and reports).

You can see from this brief sketch that we, the teachers, are keeping a tight hold on all of the important decisions, but we are still encouraging students in a number of places to ask good questions—after an initial introductory activity (i.e., "Coral Reefs" video), after the problematic scenario, and after visits from local experts. Our Inquiry Journals will be a good place for these inquiries as well as assignments.

Jill Levine, principal of the Normal Park Museum Magnet School in Chattanooga, TN calls these Travel Journals. Her students keep one per nine-week unit, and I'm sure they become part of a teacher's formative and summative assessments of students' progress (Levine, personal communication, 2007).

One of the best reasons to start the year this way, especially if we are new to inquiry, is that we have opportunities for students to pose good questions, but we aren't making a commitment to answer all of them, and we aren't making a commitment to include them in our unit objectives. We have ample time to elicit, post, and reflect on them and have several discussions about students' questions and the answers they are finding. A convenient place to record students' questions during this approach will be a Wonder Wall, where students' questions are written Post-it Notes® and stuck to a sheet of flip chart paper, so we can read and consider them during class when time is available.

This approach, therefore, is an excellent warm-up for us, instructionally and psychologically. We need time to get accustomed to students' having more input and, hence, more of a stake, in their own learning.

TEACHER-STUDENT NEGOTIATED INQUIRY

Now, proceeding to the next phase, one that involves more student voice and decision making, we might not see too vast a difference.

Here we might find the KWHLAQ process helpful. Following our initiating experience, we can ask, "Now, what do we think we know about the ocean? About life in the ocean? About ocean disasters?" These obviously would be three different questions at different times. We can take all of students' comments and map them out (see Figure 5.1).

Now, we can proceed in several ways. We can proceed to share the problematic scenario, discuss it, and ask, "What do we need to know if we are to complete this charge from the governor? What questions will help us figure out a solution?"

Fig 5.1 Long-Range Inquiry Strategy

K "What do we *think* we know about the subject?" Here we elicit and record all students' comments be they factual or, to our knowledge, misunderstandings. We want a record of their prior knowledge and we know (C. Heath & D. Heath, 2007; Marzano, Pickering, & Pollock, 2001) the efficacy for achievement of helping students identify and relate to prior knowledge. We will emphasize "What do we *think* we know?" because, as we will tell our students, we may have some misconceptions that we will acknowledge and eventually adjust.

W "What do we want and need to find out?" We are interested not only in what might have stimulated students' curiosity in our opening, initiating experiences (e.g., the coral reef videotape), but also in what students think we need to determine if we are to solve this problem or figure out the situation. Here we are challenging them to act as young scientists, historians, and so forth.

H "How will we go about finding answers to our questions?" This is an important step toward independent thinking and acting. We want students not only to ask good questions, but also to be able to figure out what kinds of resources will help them find answers. We also can ask here, "How will we go about organizing ourselves to find answers—e.g., use of time for access to resources, planning, working together, and presenting findings." This step will also involve organizing and making priority lists of our questions, combining and eliminating some.

L "What are we learning as we move along our journey of inquiry and what have we learned at the end of our journey?" It is very important to visit this question daily as we find out new information, for it will surely lead to our asking better, more specific and more general questions.

A "What action will we take as the result of our inquiry? How can we apply what we have learned?" This is an important aspect of our summative assessments because the response to this challenge demonstrates the depth of understanding of content concepts and ideas. We can apply concepts and skills to other school subjects and to our lives beyond school (see Chapter 7 on assessment).

Q "What new questions do we have as we proceed and after our study of this unit?" Obviously, with new information we develop new questions. But at the end of our unit there should be time to reflect on newer questions, both content (about oceans) and process (about asking good questions and seeking out answers) that we can carry along into future units, thus maintaining an ongoing spiral of learning.

Or we can ignore the problematic scenario and use all of the students' questions as well as our own essential questions to form the core of the unit. If we proceed in this fashion we will, obviously, be spending a lot of time organizing the students' questions for the unit and integrating them with our own. Students' questions thus become like planets orbiting around the sun of our own teacher inquiries.

These questions can become the focus for our work toward understanding the oceans of the world. Since we have done the planning just outlined, we will be ready for most questions. We can further prepare our students to inquire along certain lines by the ways in which we provide a context for learning—with the pictures/videos and the like. If we do not intend to deal with coral reefs, then we won't select that video. If we are focusing on storms and their devastation to local communities, we will provide that context.

Since we have other objectives in mind concerning ocean life and habitats, we will ask for questions about these topics as well. Or we can limit our eliciting students' questions to just the problematic scenario to simplify matters.

"WHAT DO WE DO WITH ALL THE STUDENTS' QUESTIONS?"

I am often asked this question. And what teachers have told me is that they do the following—starting at second grade and perhaps earlier:

1. Gather all of our students' questions together—on flip charts, white boards, or other means of display.

2. Group our students in whichever ways are appropriate and challenge them to examine all of the questions with an eye toward "finding those that seem to go together. Which are asking for similar kinds of information?" A good classification task.

3. Then we can ask our students to combine these questions into broader, more clearly defined (perhaps even more general) questions about the oceans—a good challenge to combine and generalize.

4. Next, we can ask them to make priority lists based on what's important to young scientists, what's interesting to them, and so forth. Here we challenge them to think critically—what's important and why? They might also identify which questions they want to research.

5. We can then post the questions students are most eager to research.

At this point, we will privately or publicly recognize that students' questions may in fact be right in line with our own essential questions, supporting ideas, and objectives. Students will more than likely ask questions that help us move toward our planned objectives (see previous and Chapter 4). We can put them all together on flip chart paper, and post them around the room for all to see.

At this stage, we can also begin asking our students, "What are good questions? What do they do? What do they look like? What do they sound like? What makes a good question?" We can use the current unit to represent their good questions. Gradually, students will see that good questions sometimes ask for more than yes/no answers; that they get us "to think" in trying to figure out problems, find out why things exist, what will happen next, and so forth. A good experience is to create a class list of good questions to ask at various times—when reading a newspaper article, examining something in nature, and considering a short story or a novel (see Chapter 6).

6. And, finally, at this stage we should ask students, "How will we go about answering our questions?" thus invoking the *H* of the KWHLAQ process.

One of the most empowering aspects of this approach is not only that students get to ask questions that they are interested in, but also have some control over how they will go about finding answers. Why ask this question?

It makes sense that we want to educate students to be able to ask good questions and be able to figure out how to answer them as well. Researching answers is just as much of a lifelong learning skill as posing questions. We enable students to figure out how to answer their own questions just as they will do at home, during summer vacation, and when they are out in the workforce raising a family.

These questions then modify our curriculum in that we must make time for them to be answered. This means we allocate time and provide access to resources for students to conduct their investigations. We've mentioned previously the large number of resources students might access: Internet Web sites like AMNH, local authorities, books, videos/DVDs, and their parents.

At given times, we must do the following:

1. Provide time weekly for students to use computers in class, visit the media center, or the computer room. Following each session, have students discuss in class what they've learned and jot down more notes and questions in their Inquiry Journals.

2. Provide time weekly for us to present more teacher-directed lessons, as appropriate, on such topics as ocean currents, global climate change/warming, preserving ocean environments, and varieties of ocean life. These topics relate to our essential questions and are foundational for students' understanding the answers to their own questions.

3. Have class discussions about what to do with their answers and new questions, modifying thereby some of their original intentions.

4. Create a class rubric with our students for evaluating our solutions and projects related to ocean storms. Students need to know what's important and how to gauge their own progress in terms of knowledge of content and inquiry and use of good language skills. Creating the rubric with them gives them a greater sense of control over their own learning (see Chapter 7).

The excitement of this unit with third, fourth, fifth, or sixth graders will obviously come from what our students are learning about their questions and about our questions.

THE MEDIA CENTER AS LOCUS OF INQUIRY

At PS 106 in Brooklyn there is a state-of-the-art media center, also known as a library. Here when students arrive, they can look up at the ceiling and find the fruits of their inquiries, for posted on the overhead are many students' questions:

- "Why do people change?
- Where does the sky end?
- Do trees need sleep?
- Why is black the color of depression?
- Do animals go to the same heaven as people?
- Where does wind come from?
- Porque hay Guerra?"

In this spectacular library, students can read, pose, and answer questions.

What a marvelous way to foster inquiry—to post it throughout the school as they do here at PS 106 (Schibsted, 2005, p. 25).

ACCESSING RESOURCES TO ANSWER QUESTIONS

In my mind I can now see pictures of Ann White's East Orange fourth graders researching their unit on rocks after using the KWHLAQ process (see Barell, 2003, Chapter 8). I made a videotape of this unit and can vividly recall students at the computer trying to figure out about different kinds of rocks ("How'd you get that!?"), students who printed pictures at home from Google or a USGS site about strange rock formations on the coast of California, and students who asked great questions of Dr. Jonathan Lincoln, my colleague from Montclair State University and chair of the Earth Science Department:

"What's the biggest rock?" (Dr. Lincoln replied, "Have you ever heard of the TV show, *3rd Rock from the Sun?* Well, that's Earth, the biggest rock.")

"What's the most important rock?" (He went on to describe large deposits of igneous rock that are mined for local road and other local and national construction projects. "Basalt—magma from volcanoes—is one of the most familiar and available rocks on Earth," Dr. Lincoln said.)

And my favorite: "If there were no volcanoes would it affect rocks?" (And Dr. Lincoln launched into a hand demonstration of a dense ocean plate subducting beneath a less dense continental plate and how that generated magma and volcanoes. His point was that moving plates strongly affect not only mountain building but also, as we've observed elsewhere, the very existence of life here on Earth. Even though we are finding some evidence of water on Mars from the two rovers, Spirit and Opportunity, Mars is now a dead planet without any plate tectonics.)

I think of Robin Cayce's fifth-grade students in Chattanooga practicing asking each other questions in preparation for venturing out into the city to interview parents and others about their World War II experiences and recollections. They practiced asking good questions, listening, and then posing follow-up questions.

Kelly Guzman's second-grade classroom comes to mind as well. They were working on a unit focusing on communities and natural disasters with a problematic scenario that called for students to figure out how to rebuild New Orleans. (See her problematic scenario at the end of the last chapter.) During the process, she received this question from one of her students:

"When interviewing, how do we get our subject to tell us more?"

As Kelly remarked, "What a great question!" and I thought, *especially for second graders*, but then we often underestimate our students' abilities.

And I recall working with several classes at PS 238 in Brooklyn where Margaret Schultz was principal. With these classes I worked for the American Museum of Natural History and would model the KWHLAQ strategy (as well as observe, think, and question—Chapters 3 and previous discussion). I brought in slides of the solar system of galaxies and, my favorite, one image of the black hole at the center of our Milky Way

Galaxy (visit www.google.com/images for "Center of Milky Way Galaxy" for some spectacular pictures).

We generated many questions and took some to the American Museum of Natural History's Hayden Planetarium to find some answers and generate more. One new question I recall from a seventh grader: "Why do black holes move through space?" She wrote some astronomers and got a satisfactory answer (because space is continuously expanding itself as the result of the Big Bang).

After visits like these, students in one fifth-grade classroom identified their culminating projects (this was before the days of problematic scenarios leading to a summative assessment) and I was delighted to see their presentations on Mars, the Hubble Space Telescope, Andromeda, and other space fascinations.

We will have more to say subsequently about assessment, but let me emphasize here that how we ask students to demonstrate their understanding of key concepts and skills depends on the kinds of initiating experiences and problematic scenarios we use at the commencement of our units.

If, as suggested previously, we decide not to initiate the unit with a problematic scenario, we can at some point during the core learning experiences present our students with this challenge: "How will you demonstrate to me that you understand answers to your and others' questions? How will we know that you understand the most important ideas within this unit on oceans of the world?" Here students will generate their own ideas for final projects and generate a rubric for personal assessment.

What will make this unit work is our ability to be open to new ideas and answers and feel somewhat comfortable with ambiguity and a little messiness. Once we engage students with the power to make some decisions, we know unpredictable events will occur and that is part of the excitement, the lure, and the satisfaction with this approach.

"Do butterflies walk?"

The KWHLAQ framework might provide you with real opportunities to challenge and engage students in new and unforeseen ways. For example, Tory Paul, a kindergarten teacher in Santa Rosa, California, often wondered about including what she considered to be students' misconceptions within a KWL framework. She recently wrote in an e-mail,

> After reading *Developing More Curious Minds*, I was taken with the KWHLAQ chart and realized this could solve my problem of how to address incorrect information, as well as add that layer of

inquiry so vital to tapping into children,s curiosity. When introducing a recent unit (Spring 2007) for our International Baccalaureate theme of Sharing The Planet, we were exploring different living things in our world. On the day our Painted Lady caterpillars arrived, we developed a K chart, but this time instead of saying, "What do we know about butterflies and caterpillars?" I asked them what do we think we know. Suddenly, this opened up everything to speculation and questioning.

Tory was now more open to speculations about butterflies, such as this one:

> When Lizette stated that the butterflies will walk, the room erupted into noisy controversy. All eyes turned to me, "Is that true? Is that right?" they all demanded. They were shocked when I admitted I didn't know either. It was a fabulous opportunity for me to turn control of the learning over to the students. Instead of our usual model of all information going from teacher to student in a one-way exchange of information, I showed the students that they had the power to discover their own answers.

Then the class asked, "How can we answer our questions?" and they concluded that they would watch the butterflies as they grew.

> We saw them extend their proboscis and drink nectar from the flowers. And then, one day it was Lizette who remembered our question and exclaimed in the middle of centers time, "They walk! The butterflies are walking!" and sure enough, there they were in their enclosure creeping about on the flowers, basking in the sun on the bottom, and sidling up to one another going around and around in a circle trying to mate. We all felt very pleased with ourselves for finding out the answer and a mood of festivity took hold of the class, as we added "Butterflies do walk!" to our recording chart. (To Paul, personal communication, 2007)

Tory opened her own thinking and that of her students when she considered, "What do we think we know?" thus allowing us to consider what we initially considered misconceptions.

INDEPENDENT STUDENT INVESTIGATIONS

At the far right of our spectrum, we have the happy condition in which we have mature students who, independently or collaboratively, can pose their own questions, conduct research, and work toward resolution.

How would we structure such students' work?

I suggest this triad of questions as a good model:

Planning

"What is our problem/question and how do we plan to respond/ answer it?" What steps do we need to take in order to organize ourselves, our personal and classroom time, and our access to in-school and beyond resources? How will we plan our analysis of information gathered, our putting together our final projects? At this stage, it is a good idea to write out our plans, including our questions, our resources, our time schedules, and our anticipated completion target dates—beginning, middle, and end. Begin to think of how you might share your findings and what you wish to be held accountable for. All of these questions will be settled in small group meetings with the teacher who will, of course, approve of the project's major question(s), its courses of action, and for what and how students will be held accountable.

Monitoring

"How well are we working toward our objectives?" This entails continual monitoring of progress, perhaps in Inquiry Journals that mark our planning and our daily progress toward resolutions/answers. In these journals we can record our new findings, new ideas, and newer questions that might modify our thoughts about final projects. While in this phase, we should be creating a self-assessment rubric in which we identify those elements for which we will be held responsible: e.g., content, inquiry process, presentation, use of English language, and ability to respond to others' questions.

These monitoring approaches will constitute our formative assessments, as students share with us their progress, difficulties, new questions, and alternative courses of action.

During this phase students will think of the many and varied ways of sharing their understandings with the whole class. I do not believe in private showings unless there are very good reasons, ones that might have to do with special students' needs or time. These alternative assessment approaches might include various written formats, including PowerPoint presentations, oral sharings with the whole class, any aesthetic means of representing what we've learned (poetry, drama, our own paintings/works in clay, or any other medium), panels, video presentations, and simulations/games. (One cautionary note: I've seen enough PowerPoint presentations to be concerned that too many of them demonstrate facility with software but not necessarily with the ideas presented therein.)

Evaluating

"How well did we do and what might we do differently next time?" Here we can use our self-assessment framework to assess our progress, how well we responded to comments at a practice session with teachers and fellow students, our modifications for improvement, and our final self-assessments. These final assessments ought to include responses to questions like these: "What did I learn about the subject I thought was really important and why? What did I learn about myself and the process of inquiry—asking a question and searching for answers? How can/will I apply what I have learned to other subjects in school and to my life outside of school?" And, finally, "What new questions do I have about the subject, myself, and about inquiry resulting from this investigation?"

Needless to say, this triad of organizational questions is also appropriate for the whole class to use during the negotiated structure we've discussed previously.

CONCLUSION

This has been a long and complex process of planning and initiating our units of inquiry. We commenced with a short vignette that some saw as too chaotic. It reminds me of a teacher's question at a recent workshop: "How do we tell the difference between chaos and inquiry?" The very question suggests that this topic had been on her mind and may, just may, have acted as an inhibiting factor in pursuing the high challenge of getting students to buy into their own learning by asking good questions. (In general, we concluded during this session that the activity I planned was engaging, loud with busy, on-task talk, and therefore, an example of inquiry that at times is quite different from students sitting quietly listening to the teacher talk.)

We've explored three different models that are each appropriate on different occasions:

- **Teacher Directed/Structured Inquiry**—This model is appropriate when we are just learning to teach or learning the subject; when we want to warm up by getting students to ask questions but do not want the responsibility for including them directly into the unit; when we aren't sure how we will manage a different kind of classroom with input from students.

- **Teacher-Student Negotiated/Guided Inquiry**—A process wherein students' questions become integrated into our unit objectives, and not just our own essential questions. This occurs when we have spent some time writing in our own Inquiry Journals (teachers and students), reflecting on our own curiosities—what fosters our curiosity, the kinds of questions we do and do not ask, and to what extent we seek answers; when we have spent some time with exploratory kinds of observe, think, and question activities using objects, pictures, and stories to foster students' questions and spent time with them figuring out what are good questions; and when we are personally comfortable in our knowledge of the subject matter and with managing a different kind of classroom, one where students will be doing more group work and following through with questions that they are really interested in. We will engage in this kind of negotiated structure when we have prepared students to work collaboratively, to listen and respond to each other and to be able to ask good questions (See Chapter 3).

- **Independent Student Investigations**—Here we may have students who are mature, good at independent and/or group work and can be trusted to work well on their own. Their work should, however, be made part of whatever unit we are working on and they should be sharing their findings with those in class as they make progress. (By the way, I have never been and am not now a proponent of pull-out programs for advanced and gifted students. If we must have such, then I hope these students will share what and how they are learning with other students who are not so fortunate to receive special attention.)

This kind of teaching isn't everybody's cup of tea. But in some schools, like those in the International Baccalaureate program (www.ibo.org), inquiry is front and center in the mission statement and in the student profile, and we must figure out ways to challenge our students to ask good questions related to our units of instruction.

PRACTICAL OPPORTUNITIES

1. Identify a unit you have taught and reconfigure it using the KWHLAQ format suggested here.

2. Take a unit you are planning and use the processes in Chapter 4 and in this chapter to plan for students to have more control over their own inquiry processes.

3. What do you see as the special challenges of each of the strategies identified in this chapter?

4. Where are you on the spectrum from Teacher Directed to Independent Study? Where would you like to be? What steps can you take in order to arrive at your destination?

5. What questions do you have about these approaches? Where can you find answers?

6. To what extent can and do you engage in long-range planning with colleagues? (Please feel free to share your questions with me at jbarell@nyc.rr.com)

7. What do you think Tory Paul's realization adds to the process of working with students?

"Why Are Mountains Necessary?"

The Nature of Good Questions

INFORMAL WONDER TALK

One morning I sat down with a group of kindergartners at Whittier International Elementary School in Minneapolis to read a story about Antarctica, a subject about which I can become very passionate because of my own journeys to that continent when I was serving in the U.S. Navy.

We all sat in a circle on the rug and I began to model my own inquisitiveness by telling students about visiting the polar regions. That usually gets them a little more interested in the subject, as teachers have noted: "You established a personal connection with the subject." I told them briefly about why I went—out of curiosity about the land, the many explorers, the animals, the weather and discovering new places (Barell, 2007b).

I showed them the large picture book called *Antarctica* (Cowcher, 1990) and began to wonder aloud about the two Emperor penguin heads on the cover: "What kinds of animals are these? Where are they found? How big are they? What do they eat?" and "How in the world do you suppose they survive in such cold weather?"

Then we begin to read the story, and as we moved from picture to picture the story of *The March of the Penguins* unfolds (even though this story was written prior to that Academy Award winning documentary). Soon and without prompting students were expressing their own curiosities rather informally: "I wonder why the penguins are different sizes . . . You have hair on your wrist, why? Do you think penguins have hair or fur on their heads?"

This is an example of what we've previously (see Chapter 1) identified as "wonder talk," an expression of curiosities expressed within informal settings like this one: sitting in a circle reading a book.

Wonder talk occurs whenever we are having an informal conversation, say in the front seat of a car driving through a park, en route to the train station, or in the kitchen preparing a meal. We are discussing events, objects, or observations and sometimes one of us says, "You know, I wonder . . ." or "Maybe . . . perhaps . . . do you think?"

As we just mentioned, these are good questions because the students really wanted to know the answers. These questions led the teacher, after my visit, to share with students pictures of volcanoes and other natural phenomena and these led to more questions, such as the one geologists still ponder today: "What causes volcanoes to explode?"

MORE FORMAL INQUIRY SESSIONS

In another Minneapolis school (Earle Brown Elementary IB World School), I was working with a group of fourth graders on the topic of natural resources. My purpose was to model various inquiry approaches for teachers who were sitting in the rear of the room, and I began by sharing with the

> "Then one student, Howard, asked this question, 'Why are mountains necessary?' I was surprised by the question, but quickly wrote it down."

students pictures of Antarctica, where I told students I had visited. I wanted to establish that personal connection with a territory and its resources, among which are coal and perhaps oil, in addition to various minerals and meteorites (some of them Martian). We discussed what we might find in Antarctica. Their responses included penguins, whales, and birds; lots of ice and icebergs; climate and mountain ranges. Maps and photos helped stimulate their interest.

We then proceeded with the initial stages of a KWHLAQ: "What do we think we already know about natural resources?" and the students shared their prior knowledge about coal, various minerals like gold and silver, water, and air/wind.

Then it was time for students to pose questions and they had many, including, "How do you make gold and silver?" I immediately thought of the ancient alchemists who labored over this very question without success.

Then one student, Howard, asked this question, "Why are mountains necessary?" I was surprised by the question, but quickly wrote it down.

Then came another question from Kamouri sitting next to him, "What if there were no clouds?" And I wrote that down.

My purpose here is to set before us a number of questions like these to challenge us to figure out something about the nature of "good questions." What constitutes good opening wonderings that lead to finding things out?

Without reference to grade levels and the nature of the students who posed these questions, here are some others for us to think about. These are all questions posed by Pre–K through Grade 6 students:

Sample Questions

- Do butterflies walk?
- The sun is a gas. Does that mean that light is also a gas?
- Why are mountains necessary?
- What if there were no clouds?
- How did the Liberty Bell crack?
- Why are religions so important to people?
- Why can't everybody believe in the same thing [religion]?
- Why are school buses always yellow?
- How do the police and firefighters get paid?
- How did people become leaders in ancient civilizations?
- How did cultures originate?
- Will we ever have another ice age?
- If there were no volcanoes, would it affect rocks?
- Why do penguins walk so funny?
- What's an eardrum?
- What kinds of clothing did ancient Romans wear?
- Are modern buildings in the United States mainly from ancient Roman designs?
- When the Incas were using dots for numbers, were they doing multiplication like we do today?
- Why do flares shoot out from the sun?
- Does the president have the right to create a draft for military purposes?
- How do we know about protons, neutrons, and electrons if we can't see them?

All of these questions were asked by students in various elementary schools around the country. Now, how do we determine if they are "good questions"?

REFLECTIVE PAUSE

Reread these questions and select those you think are "good." Then ask yourself the critical thinking question: "What makes these 'good' questions? What criteria am I using to select some and not others?"

One definition of critical thinking we are using here is that from my former colleague, Matthew Lipman (1988), the developer of the Philosophy for Children Program at Montclair State University. Here's Matt's definition: "critical thinking is skillful, fully responsible thinking that facilitates judgments because it (1) relies on criteria, (2) is self-correcting, and (3) is sensitive to context" Here we are asking for the criteria with which you made your judgment or drew your conclusions.

When I first started working with inquiry years ago, I asked teachers this very question: "What makes a good question?"

One respondent said, "A good question is any one you want an answer to."

And this makes sense. We ask a wide variety of questions in our daily lives, at home, at work and while shopping, taking clothes to the cleaner, gardening, or attending to any number of vocations and avocations. Our curiosities, as Lindfors (1999) points out, might come in the form of wonderings (not formal questions) such as "Maybe . . . perhaps . . . I don't understand . . . What if . . . ? and I wonder why. . . ." Lindfors' research suggests that such "acts of inquiry" might be what she calls "information gathering" (rather closed, convergent product oriented requests). Or they might reflect "play with possibilities" (p. 37) explorations of mysteries, incongruities that we share with a trusted partner, someone on whom we impose an expectation of help to make sense of the world and our experiences.

Our wonderings about how the world works are most often genuine attempts to understand. In either of Lindfors' categories, it seems as if we want information in order to understand and to make something meaningful. Our search for understanding is motivated by the desire to close those gaps in our learning, in our understanding, that give rise to curiosities (H. Heath & C. Heath, 2007).

So, what are other ways of considering our questions and wonderings, ways of figuring out their significance, their meaningfulness? (Note: We can and should at appropriate times ask our students, "What makes a good question?")

Here are some different ways of looking at questions:

1. Are they "authentic," as one teacher asked recently about a modeling experience in the same school just described. He meant, I think, that students genuinely wanted to know the answer and were not merely completing an adult-taught stem such as Who?, What?, When?, Why?, and How? They weren't playing a game of "Guess what's on the teacher's mind?" Does the student's question result from a spontaneous desire to know?

What are some indicators of "genuineness"? you ask. Well, perhaps these might be some considerations: (1) the occasion of asking (Tommy comes into class one morning and says, "You know, Mrs. Brown, I was wondering . . ."); (2) the setting (Alice is in her reading group and says, "I really don't understand why Franklin is scared—I'm not!"—*Franklin in the Dark*); (3) the look of puzzlement (Jennifer sits in class listening to a discussion with a furrowed brow and a quizzical look on her face); (4) writings in Inquiry Journals ("You know, maybe . . . "); (5) conversations at home reported by student and/or parents; (6) interest that persists over time ("I'm still wondering about . . .").

What other indicators of genuineness come to your mind?

Other criteria for "good" questions might include the following:

2. To what degree do these questions challenge us to think deeply about an issue, a problem, or a curiosity? In other words, which questions give us short answers found by reading, for example, and which questions ask us to think deeply about a problem or issue and do something with that information such as think at Levels II and III of the Three Story Intellect (see Figure 3.2).

3. Which questions might reflect research findings positively related to student achievement? For example, comparison/contrast questions (see Marzano, Pickering, & Pollock, 2001).

4. Which questions help us move toward our curricular objectives? (See Chapter 3.)

5. And which questions help us use information, to act on it, and to apply it to new, different kinds of situations? Or which questions open new dimensions of investigation we hadn't even thought of before—with a student just wondering about what fascinates him or her?

Let's look at the sample questions using the second point made here, the degree to which the questions challenge us to think productively.

Another way of looking at this is to determine the nature of the intellectual task presented with each question, which is not always a simple matter.

Question: ***"Why are mountains necessary?"*** When I heard this question, I was thrilled because of what I saw in it—not that Howard had the same ideas in his mind. To me this question asks about the role mountains play in the development of our "dynamic Earth," as geologists call it. If we answer the question completely, we'll think not only about how mountains form from the movements of tectonic plates and how these plates have shaped Earth as it is today, but also about their significant role in fostering life as we know it (Ward & Brownlee, 2000).

Thus, this question, from a special education student in fourth grade, challenges us to figure out causal relationships, to explain the dynamics of connections and interrelationships among various Earth elements. This, to me is a most complex question, even though this student probably did not see it this way. What did he mean by it? I'm not sure, because we didn't ask him. He might have looked at a map of the United States, at the dark brown streak representing the Rocky Mountains and wondered, "Why are they there?" This reminds me of a question philosophers often ask: "Why is there something here, and not nothing?" Why are things as they are rather than otherwise? Too often we take things—a lot of things—for granted. And this student's question challenges us to ask tough questions about what we see before us and take for granted.

Let us here refer to the Three Story Intellect (see Figure 3.2). This framework, built from the work of Benjamin Bloom and his Taxonomy of Cognitive Objectives, provides a neat structure with which to gauge the intellectual demands of our questions.

> Level I Gathering information
>
> Level II Processing gathered information, thereby clarifying and making it more understandable; analyzing and drawing reasonable conclusions
>
> Level III Applying and using said information

It seems evident from several research sources that we must engage students at Levels II and III, not just at Level I, for them to understand and be able to apply and use data constructively (Mayer, 1975, 1989; Bransford, Brown, & Cocking, 2000; Newman & Associates, 1996; Marzano, et al., 2001; Marzano, 2003).

What I usually tell teachers when viewing and using the Three Story Intellect is that we must challenge students to think at Levels II and III if we expect them to learn, understand, remember, and be able to use the information and ideas they are working with. Anything less may merely be regurgitation of mindless information.

Howard's question, therefore, appears clearly to be a Level II question—seeking to understand causes—and, therefore, a good question because it challenges us to think—to gather information, analyze it, search for connections and causes, perhaps engage in "If this, then that" kind of thinking, and draw reasonable conclusions.

Regardless of the level of question (and that is not of paramount importance here), Howard's question leads him and his classmates to understand how mountains form (from the movements of plates) and what these geological structures tell us about our ever-changing planet.

Question: ***"How did the Liberty Bell crack?"*** This question from a five-year-old student seems like a Level I question on the face. We're searching for historical information that will explain why we have a certain condition today. When the student found out that there had been a fault in the design of the bell that caused it to crack while being cast, the student was disappointed. "But, Mrs. Davis, I asked a really good question...and I didn't get a really good answer! I thought something cool happened to it like a cannonball hit it or something!" the student replied. Ahh! The lesson learned. ***Not all interesting questions have interesting answers!***

So, Level I, case closed? Perhaps not. What if we wanted to pursue this matter further, to sleuth down the root causes. Yes, there was a design flaw, according to the information Mrs. Davis and her students uncovered. But what's the next set of questions?

> Who designed the Liberty Bell?
>
> What was the nature of the design flaw?
>
> Why did the designer make this mistake?

We can, it seems, dig deeper and in some instances we, indeed, should not accept the first answer—"design flaw." This answer should create a whole host of new questions that might lead us to some fascinating surprises about casting metals in the eighteenth century, about patterns or design and the like.

Still a Level I question? Perhaps, but one that could easily lead to close analysis of these related factors, but probably not for a five-year-old. Consider what happens when we do not pursue such questions to their deeper roots—NASA has been accused of doing just this with such deficiencies as leaks from the O-Rings that, sadly, led to the loss of Space Shuttle Challenger in 1986.

Question: ***"How did/and do cultures originate?"***

I promptly wrote this sixth grader's question on the white board as his classmates peppered me with inquiries about cultures, their origins, their different elements, and even why we use the word "culture" itself.

Clearly, we are searching for origins here; we are looking for causes. Is this a cut-and-dry situation of looking up the answer in a textbook, thereby casting this question as a Level I: gathering information?

Those of us who have ever studied history or are keen on reading history today might agree that determining why and how human creations (or natural events) originated, and how we got to where we are today considering a wide variety of cultures might not be an easy matter.

In the first place, maybe no one has asked this question and perhaps there's no research on just how various cultures originated. Maybe, also, there are conflicting interpretations. For that's what they will be, somebody's reasoned conclusion about any one culture, starting from Paleolithic times through Neolithic, up to cultures today—urban, suburban, rural, mountain, tundra, and so on.

And with any conclusion about history or anthropology, we can look at whatever evidence there is and generate alternate points of view. We know, for example, that early hominids developed stone tools during the Paleolithic era dating back to 2.5 million years ago. Such tools such as flakes suitable for cutting were chipped from rocks with high concentrations of silicon dioxide, chert, or flint. Now, did human culture develop from this ability to work collaboratively during hunting prey? Or was the fact of our bipedalism, walking upright and exploring beyond the savannas also a key factor together with our burgeoning brain size? (For more information search "Stone Tools," and "Paleolithic" on www.google.com.) In other words, did culture precede the use of stone tools and our bipedalism or result from them? (This may depend, of course, on our definition of "culture." Whenever working with such a concept, we will work with our students to define initially and then refine our definition as we learn more.)

We may not be able to come to an agreed upon answer to this question, but the inquiry process will be fascinating!

Not all questions, therefore, that search for good reasons will result in a cut-and-dried answer. Many Level II questions searching for explanations can lead us to hypothesizing in history and anthropology just as we do in science. This will demand we draw conclusions and use good evidence, data, and information to support these conclusions. (Consider this question: "Why don't all people believe the same thing—in terms of their religion?")

This question is also a good example of one that might lead us directly to consider a curricular objective we've identified as we webbed out the concept "Culture" in our planning of this unit, planning that would lead toward generating a problematic scenario suitable for opening and closing the unit as well as our unit objectives.

For another example, Liz Debrey at Whittier International Elementary School in Minneapolis spent time with her fourth and fifth graders (a combined class) challenging them to sort their questions about world religions to determine which ones were closely aligned with their unit objects, ones that related to beliefs, the nature of gods, ceremonies/rituals, and other similar concepts.

WHAT ARE "GOOD QUESTIONS"?

During this same unit on religion, Liz asked her students to examine their questions and determine what made a "good question." A good question, they said,

- Has more than one answer
- Has a very deep meaning
- Contains exciting words because that makes someone want to look for the answer
- Doesn't have a yes or no answer
- Has more than one answer, and is something you wonder about
- Is hard to answer and takes a lot of thinking to understand the question
- Is about something you can research
- Takes a long time to figure out
- Has meaning and details in the answer and should make sense
- Is one that I keep thinking about but still don't know the answer
- Makes you think, know, and wonder
- Is not one that everybody already knows the answer to

These average fourth/fifth graders have generated a list that could be used as a set of criteria for all their unit questions. They can and should be posted around the room and subsequently modified as students become more adept at asking and analyzing their inquiries.

What would happen if you asked your students to identify what makes a "good question"?

REFLECTIVE PAUSE

Look at the remaining sample questions and decide which you think are highly challenging intellectually. Which lead us toward complex Levels II and III of the Three Story Intellect and why do you think so?

How do we recognize the good ideas/concepts within questions?

What concepts do we find in some of our sample questions?

- Here are a few:
- Culture
- Human creativity
- Liberty
- Human tool making
- Solar system
- Eardrums and other parts of our auditory system
- Nature of religion and its beliefs/ceremonies
- Leaders and leadership
- Clouds and other meteorological phenomena
- Mountains and other landforms
- Subatomic particles and their nature
- Federal government powers
- Systems of education

Why is it important to recognize these concepts within our questions?

One clear reason is that we want students to begin thinking productively about key concepts and ideas within each of our units. That's why we webbed as many in Chapter 3 as we could think of. We want students to think about big ideas and concepts because they are powerful; we can often generalize from concepts to a wide variety of situations. If we know about culture in one area, we can apply basic principles to all other cultures (not that they will be the same, but they will face similar challenges within their given environments (e.g., the indigenous populations in the Arctic, the Sahara, New York, and Moscow and farmlands around the world).

These concepts will lead us to consider our essential questions and contributing ideas. Perhaps we will not think of all of them. For example, clouds might have been part of our concept map for natural resources because they produce rain, a clear resource (**"What if there were no clouds?"**). But perhaps their absence hadn't even been considered making this question one of "What iffing?" into the future, projecting and critically analyzing possible consequences. This is one of fascination and worth investigating (given sufficient time and resources).

Learning about concepts fosters learning and application of learning to wider circumstances. We know that students' developing their own concept maps can facilitate their cognitive development as well as their academic achievement. What such exercises do is help students delineate all the associations they make with the words "car," "cell," "Canada," or "hero," for example. They can also extend the network of meaningful relationships webbed out by the student (see Copple, Sigel, & Saunders, 1984; Johnson, 1975; Novak, 1998). So, the more practice we give students in identifying key concepts such as "culture" and "cell," the more meaningful these concepts become and, meaningful learning is certainly one of our key goals for all education: the deep and extensive understanding of important concepts and ideas.

And the more practice we give students in analyzing concepts for example, by comparing and contrasting and drawing conclusions about similarities and differences, the more we deepen their understanding of these concepts and, therefore, foster their academic achievement and cognitive growth (Copple et al., 1984).

ANOTHER WAY OF LOOKING AT QUESTIONS

During one of my visits, Liz Debrey of Whittier International in Minneapolis and her colleagues were working with groups of fourth- and fifth-grade students on an ancient civilization unit. After showing students various illustrations of Greeks going about their daily commerce within view of the Acropolis, men in togas in Rome, and similar pictures from ancient Egypt, Liz and her colleagues had a variety of student questions:

- Is this Rome? Egypt?
- I wonder if they're thinking, looking at maps, talking?
- Are some people sad?

All team members wanted to help students develop deeper questions and ones that would help students respond to the problematic scenario. This scenario called for students to examine a civilization of choice, select several cultural elements, and compare them with what they see today. In order to help students think more deeply, I introduced Figure 6.1 directly, giving each group of students a copy of this different orientation to questioning and, using a concrete example from their school lives (e.g., a problem in the cafeteria), leading them through the questions at the twelve, three, six, and nine o'clock positions.

I then asked students to go back to their pictures and their original questions and see if they could find cultural elements that were similar to what they see in their town and in Minneapolis today. In other words, I wanted them to find significant elements and make comparisons. Liz and her colleagues were immensely satisfied with their new questions, because not only did they look for similarities in terms of fashion, marketing, architecture, and use of leisure time, but also some of their best conclusions were drawn from the differences they found.

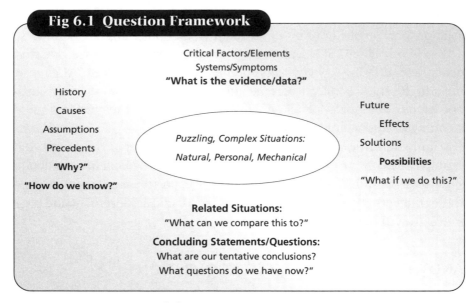

Fig 6.1 Question Framework

Critical Factors/Elements
Systems/Symptoms
"What is the evidence/data?"

History

Causes

Assumptions

Precedents

"Why?"

"How do we know?"

Puzzling, Complex Situations:

Natural, Personal, Mechanical

Future

Effects

Solutions

Possibilities

"What if we do this?"

Related Situations:
"What can we compare this to?"

Concluding Statements/Questions:
What are our tentative conclusions?
What questions do we have now?"

Here are some of their newer questions:

- "Are modern buildings in the United States mainly from ancient Roman designs?"
- "How do birth and death rituals in ancient times compare with our birth and death rituals today?"
- "How did trading goods in ancient times get us to buying and selling goods today?"

Liz wrote me later about their projects:

John, their papers are incredible! This is the best work I have ever had in ten years of teaching. The inquiry process was so meaningful to them. They were finding out answers to what THEY were genuinely curious about . . . They were so thoughtful, and well written, for a first time research paper/project this year (November/December). Their reflections on their favorite parts and what they learned were also very thoughtful. . . . I realized the differences are so important . . . Some of them wrote about the differences, and it seemed like they learned almost more about the meaning of it all by noting the differences (Debrey, personal communication, December, 2006).

What is clear is that if we challenge students to think like young historians, cultural anthropologists—young professionals—and if we provide them with time, resources, and encouragement, they will live up to our highest expectations.

"WHAT DO WE NEED TO FIND OUT?"

Another way of looking at good questions to ask, "What would a scientist ask about earthquakes?" or "What would an author ask about a character in a story?" These kinds of questions take us back to the KWHLAQ format described in Chapter 5. Recall that we can ask, "What do we think we know about volcanoes, raising pigs, about whales or problems with numbers in them?"

Then, at some point, we want students to think about what they are curious about. When doing this unit with fifth graders studying the Age of Exploration, they thought they knew a lot about Columbus—his home, his relationship to Queen Isabella [one student thought they were married!], his ships, and so on. Then we asked what this generation of prior knowledge has brought up in terms of what they didn't know—their knowledge gaps.

They wanted to know about the ships and their sizes, the number of crew, how many were criminals released from prison (not many as I recall), and what Columbus discovered or thought he'd discovered. What I didn't ask at the time was, "What do we need to know about these voyages if we are thinking like historians?" Had I challenged the students in this fashion we might have, over time, developed questions such as

- What led them to sail west (causation)?
- What were the effects of their voyages (consequences)?
- What were these voyages like in our time (comparisons)?
- Who were the leaders?

During workshops, I often engage teachers in thinking this way about objects or pictures drawn from science or cultural studies to generate the questions a professional would ask. Then I ask them to examine a series of claims made by various persons and ask the kinds of questions we should ask if we want to act on these conclusions. For this exercise, I am using John McPeck's definition of critical thinking: ". . . critical thought involves a certain skepticism, or suspension of assent, towards a given statement, established norm or mode of doing things." (McPeck, 1981, p. 6)

The key thought here is that critical thinking reflects a "certain skepticism," a willingness to withhold judgment, to doubt, and to ask good questions before we accept or believe what we're told.

REFLECTIVE PAUSE

The following is a list of claims made by actual people (except one) who wish us to believe what they say. What questions would you ask about any one of them? Once you have a set of questions, determine which ones you can generalize to apply to all of the others. And finally, see if you can create a mnemonic or acronym for your questions. Our purpose here is to identify a set of good questions we can ask about a wide variety of events/issues/stories/products in order to understand them.

> "*Charlotte's Web* is the best book in the whole world!"
>
> "It's 'very likely' that humans have caused/observed global warming of the past fifty years."
>
> "We lacked imagination . . . and what we must do is to institutionalize, routinize, [and] bureaucratize the use of imagination."
>
> "Are you getting enough whole grain in your diet? Chances are, you're not. Recent studies show nine out of ten Americans fall short of getting the recommended three servings of whole grain each day."
>
> "All snowflakes are unique. (All grains of sand are unique.)"
>
> "Get Reliable and Save Big This Year—Verizon Wireless."
>
> "The Democrats/Republicans will win the next election."
>
> "Congress was absent during the Vietnam War, and it didn't ask the tough questions and . . . we lost 58,000 Americans and lost a war and humiliated this nation . . . As long as I am here . . . I am going to do whatever I can to make sure that isn't going to happen."

This exercise (designed for adults in a workshop, and not for children) is intended to focus our attention on good, general questions that apply to a variety of situations. My intention is to model a process of being skeptical and then to determine which questions and concerns can apply in general to experiences we have had with polluted ponds, stories in the newspapers that deal with poor health care facilities, a good novel, or a work of art. Can our students learn to identify their own general questions in this way without our having to teach them the acronyms we have created?

I believe we can and think it's important for us to challenge our students to think about what young scientists, novelists, historians, mathematicians, and artists need to ask about complex, perplexing, and difficult situations.

My own acronym for what I'd like to think about under these circumstances is SEADS:

S Source. Who said this and why?

E Evidence. What data/information do we have to support the claim?

A Assumptions. What assumptions are we making about telephone service, wars, dietary fiber, and so on?

D Definitions. What words do we need to define, such as "best," "whole grain," and "reliable."

S Slant. What kind of slant, bias, or special/personal interest does the speaker/author have in making this claim? What is his or her motivation?

When I work with educators, I prefer to have them generate their own sets of good questions because I believe it's more important for them to have ownership of their questions just as I hope their students will have.

Kerry Faber is a fourth-grade teacher in Edmonton, Alberta. What makes her class a little different is that she teaches only students with special needs—students with a one- to two-year delay in reading. After a workshop, I asked Kerry if she thought her students could develop an acronym of questions that would apply generally to a wide variety of situations. She accepted the challenge and here's what her students came up with while working on a unit on pirates:

I - Information?

W - Who/what does it involve?

O - Opinion or fact?

N - Not real or real? Or natural impact (like a meteorite hitting Earth)

D - Do we know something/enough about this?

E - Evidence? Elements?

R - Real?

Kerry said she had to help them with the "O" in I WONDER,

> I chose the acronym letters for the framework. It made sense to them because this is the way many of them are learning to ask more thought-provoking questions. I also guided them with the question for "O". I want this to be something they look at a lot AND they have to be given at least a piece of a model to get them started. (K. Faber, personal communication, April, 2007)

With her students, Kerry also challenged them to learn the Three Story Intellect (Figure 3.2). When one of the major student observations during a unit on pirates ("What we think we know") was "Pirates were stupid!," she asked her students to ask questions at each of the different levels of this model. Here are their first attempts:

1   I wonder if he is a captain (looking at a picture of pirates)?

3   I wonder what would happen the next time they bury treasure (in the same place)?

2   I wonder why they bury treasure?

2   Based on what we know, how are these pirates the same?

3   Is this a good example of Captain Jack?

2   Why was he killed?

Kerry concluded,

Now that they have been introduced to the framework, I can ask them to judge what level of questions they ask me each day to heighten their awareness of the value of good questions that can't be easily answered with a "yes" or "no." (K. Faber, personal communication, April, 2007)

So our students—even those who are significantly challenged—can ask good questions and figure out an arrangement (an acronym or mnemonic) that they can use, remember, and modify as necessary.

AGAIN, WONDER TALK

We opened this chapter with children's wonderings about fur on penguins, their sizes, and why they are of various colors—Emperors and Adelies have different markings. If we follow Lindfors' (1999) categorization of inquiry acts into "Information gathering" and wonderings, then some of these questions seem to fall into the latter category (p. 38). Wonderings about size, fur, and colors are not merely seeking information as we might define it, but seem to be attempts to figure out some of the obvious incongruities such as the differences in size between the Emperor penguins (about three or more feet tall) and the smaller Adelies (about eighteen inches or less).

Why do I say this? Because these questions remind me of other young children's questions about these fascinating creatures: "Why do they walk so funny?" One child said, "Because that's the way God made them."

Well, okay. But then I got them to experience walking as if their ankles were tied together.

We aren't going to introduce religious ideas of creation, evolutionary development, adaptation, and survival needs in kindergarten, but at some point we can begin to speak with children about needs creatures have to survive in different environments.

"Why are they black and white?" is a question I've heard from adults. The answer appears to relate to the birds' need to blend in with the dark waters of Antarctica when they are swimming. The white on their bellies camouflages them from killer whales and leopard seals swimming below and looking up toward the sky.

The same group of kindergartners with whom I read the penguin story later, via e-mail, asked, "Why do volcanoes explode?" I searched various geological sites via Google and, lo and behold, that question is one at the core of science's analysis of these amazing structures. It seems as if there's some disagreement, but, generally, volcanoes do or do not explode depending on the composition of gases within the magma and the build up of pressure within the cone of the volcano (or the presence of a blockage).

By the way, a group of special education fourth graders with whom I read a story about landforms, including volcanoes, had the same question about causality. So we can't always tell a kindergartner's question from a fourth grader's, or at least, I cannot. The kindergartners had many observations (identifying what they called "aurora borealis" in a picture— actually, "aurora australis," or southern lights), and lots of questions partly because they'd seen the films *The March of the Penguins*, *Eight Below*, and *Happy Feet*.

Questions often come from what we already know. We need to have some background knowledge about a topic before we begin to explore incongruities or mysteries. That's why it's so important to provide background through initiating experiences or anticipatory sets (see Chapter 4). C. Heath and D. Heath (2007) call this providing a context for new knowledge, a context within which we can recognize our knowledge gaps.

CONCLUSION

We have examined several different points of view with which to examine our own questions and students' questions. Using the Three Story Intellect can help us classify questions, which will foster our own understanding of what students are asking. We want students to be asking good Level I, II, and III questions, and not merely those that seek to gather information. This is a very key process that does indeed foster inquiry. And we also want students to become more aware of the important concepts outlined in our curricula and state content standards; the more aware they are of these concepts and the more they work with them to extend their meaningfulness, the more we will foster understanding and student achievement.

However, perhaps of equal or greater importance is our working with students to help them frame sets of good questions topic—questions that can guide their own inquiries in a purposeful manner. Yes, we can teach them all these questions using teacher-made stems, but I believe that their own ideas and curiosities can be used to much better benefit, for example, in Kerry Faber's "IWONDER" model.

What we are attempting, after all, is to help our students think for themselves whenever they encounter those situations fraught with doubt, difficulty, and uncertainty. What do I need to find out and why?

PRACTICAL OPPORTUNITIES

1. When can you engage your students in informal wonder talk? What kinds of wonderings do they have?

2. What do your students think are "good" questions? Have you posted examples of good questions around the room for easy reference and modification throughout the year?

3. How do you work with your students to assess the quality of their questions? To what degree can they tell you which questions are good and why?

4. How can you use the Three Story Intellect or the graphic organizer to help students ask different, perhaps more complex questions?

5. Can you work with your students to generate a mnemonic device or acronym (like but different from "SEADS") for good questions that relate to various kinds of complex problems?

6. To what extent do your students record their wonderings and content questions in their Inquiry/Wonder Journals and periodically reflect on them? What are they learning about their ability to ask good questions?

"How Do We Know They Understand?"

7

The worst evaluation experience I've had was sitting down in New York City on a Thursday night to figure out what to ask my students on Friday about the play we'd just read. The best experience was challenging students to find any art form with which to express the depth and quality of their understanding of *Othello*. I received a lengthy sonnet about Desdemona, a marvelous cartoon of Iago, and a full-length sonata composed by Todd Van Beveren to play in class on his treasured viola (Barell, 1995). The latter experience brought to bear on our assessment experiences the concept of determining the degree to which students understand what they've been studying.

One of the best examples of assessing for understanding comes from Judy Frohman's second-grade classroom in Livingston, New Jersey. When I visited her, she showed me a wide variety of students' writings that demonstrated their understanding of important concepts. One that struck me was related to what we would call the Bernoulli principle of moving air. This principle states that as air moves quickly over an air foil (an airplane wing), it creates a slight vacuum on that surface. It is this vacuum that results in the lift (pressure from below the wing) that allows the plane to take off and stay in the air.

Mrs. Frohman asked her students at the end of the unit to "Choose either air, water, or solar forces and write a paragraph describing what you have learned about that force. Include any experiments we have done, and remember to explain how and why the experiment worked." Here's what Claire wrote:

> I would like to write about air. We had an airplane contest. Our
> planes flew because the air under our plane had a high presher

because it was skuooshed under the wing of our airplanes. The air under our airplane wanted to go to the lower preshure which is the upper side of the airplane . . . which is above the wing. (Frohman, personal communication, 2006)

Claire understands the pressure differential between the underside and the upper portion of the wing and that air on top is at a lower pressure and this creates pressure differential resulting in what we call lift. I was amazed when I first read Claire's paragraph because I had spent so much time as an adult trying to understand this principle, especially as it related to what allows a sailboat to sail into the wind—the sail acts as an airfoil in the same way that the wing of an airplane does.

ESSENTIALS OF GOOD ASSESSMENT

What we see here includes how a good teacher makes an abstract concept very concrete—by holding a flying contest with paper airplanes as well as direct teaching about a principle. Recall C. Heath and D. Heath's (2007) principles of "stickiness": making an idea simple, concrete, contrary to expectations (how can a very heavy vehicle fly?), and involved with emotion and story.

Her example also suggests the varied ways we can determine the degree to which students really understand a concept—using two different modes of assessment: draw a picture and write a paragraph giving examples. It was the paragraph that I found especially intriguing because it's what I used with my *Othello* assessment—together with the poem, sonata, and cartoon, students wrote an essay explaining how they arrived at their work of art.

Thus, we have these principles:

1. Use multiple means of assessment (e.g., writing, drawing, acting out, creating a product) that use as many senses as students use to acquire information. This also includes formative and summative assessments. Claire was given two ways of sharing understanding: drawing and writing. She might have also explained her understanding orally or acted them out.

2. Assess for the depth and quality of students' understanding. This means that the assessment does far more than tell us that students have information. It tells us that they can use it productively.

3. Provide students with choices within the assessment experiences. They also should have input into how they will be assessed.

4. Ensure that students understand at the beginning of a unit what they will be expected to know and be able to do; hence, the value of a problematic scenario.

5. Challenge students to think about what they have learned—to translate knowledge into action—in what Grant Wiggins (1998) has called an "authentic assessment," using Levels II and III of the Three Story Intellect (Figure 3.2).

Let us briefly examine each of these principles before sharing more examples of excellent assessment experiences.

Using Multiple Experiences

Traditionally, we think of the test on Friday. That's the day we will determine if students have learned what we expect them to have learned. Now, however, we think of all the different ways in which we can learn what students have taken in and processed. We have pre-assessments and formative and summative assessments—all of which might use different formats, from writing, speaking, drawing, taking quizzes, participating in class discussions, writing essays, doing projects, keeping Inquiry Journals, and creating PowerPoint presentations. When we ask students, "What do we think we already know about the oceans of the world?" we are conducting an assessment. If we ask students to complete their own concept maps of this exercise, webbing all prior knowledge, then we can return to this map and create other maps every week during a six- to nine-week unit. By the end of the unit, we will have a graphic example of what students think they're learning about oceans. We can keep six separate maps or have students use different colors to differentiate what they've learned from what they thought they already knew.

Asking this question, of course, will also reveal misunderstandings like the following I received from Upper Montclair, New Jersey, fifth graders several years ago as we mapped out what we thought we knew about the Age of Exploration and, in particular, Columbus' voyages: "He had red hair . . . was married to Queen Isabella . . . lived in England . . . brought a lot of criminals along on his ships . . . didn't know where he was . . ."

I dutifully wrote all of these responses on the chalkboard. (Remember Tory Paul's acceptance of what students *think* they know.) It was only a few minutes into the session when several students challenged some of the misconceptions about Columbus' birthplace and his marriage to Isabella. (Afterward I did say that I'd just seen the ship's logs and some of his writings at an exhibit 42nd Street Library in New York City and that his handwriting did look quite similar to Isabella's.) And we now know that there were, in fact, few criminals on board.

As we challenge students with a problematic scenario, their questions will also give us good pre-assessments of their inquiry abilities and their prior knowledge. Their questions reveal the knowledge gaps that they are uncomfortable with and want to close through investigations. As we move through the unit, we will have occasion for students to engage in the following experiences that can serve as formative assessments:

- Writing in their Inquiry Journals
- Discussions of what we are learning, what they are finding in their search for answers to their own questions
- New questions students are asking
- Weekly written assignments that might ask students to tell us what has been most important so far, what they're struggling with, and what they want to know more about
- Judicious use of homework—work planned to advance what we've done in class not merely to grind out countless responses or solutions
- Rehearsal of project presentations to achieve feedback from students

There are so many different varieties of assessment experiences and we've mentioned a few: written work, journals, demonstrations, panels, artistic creations such as drawings, paintings, music, poetry, dramatizations, PowerPoint presentations, and many others.

Using a variety of assessment experiences is very important because not all students think and behave alike. Not all of us are good writers, speakers, and artists. We tap into different strengths when we use a variety of experiences. Copple, Sigel, and Saunders (1984) speak convincingly of challenging students to find multiple ways of representing their ideas. By "representational competence" they refer to the different ways we share our understanding of "cow," "home," and "love." We stretch students' thinking by engaging them in using varied forms of self-expression, for example, language, music, pictures, and gestures (p. 20). Students "construct" their reality (and knowledge) through these different modes of representation. "Knowledge is the result of this active process of construction" (p. 18). (Some commentators on education decry "constructivism" as purporting to represent students' creating whatever they wish, as if there were no correct answers. I accept the Copple et al.'s formulation of constructing our understandings of any concept, concrete or abstract, as an essential part of the learning process, one requiring thoughtful engagement at Levels II and III, not merely taking in and repeating information somewhat mindlessly.)

As students work through a unit on community helpers, natural resources, or the various forms of government, for example, they are constructing their own internal meanings. When we challenge them, over time, to express these meanings in a variety of external forms, we are challenging them to share understandings and, thereby, make their knowledge far more meaningful.

Performing Our Understandings

Several years ago, I was working with a group of teachers, asking them to identify their instructional needs. Barbara M'Gonigle, a high school math teacher, said, "My students can get the right answer but they do not understand what it means. When I ask them to explain an answer, all they can do is parrot back what I've said or what's in the textbook."

This observation started Barbara and me on a most challenging journey during which we explored a wide variety of ways in which her students could demonstrate that they understood what they were learning. What do we mean by "understanding" what you're learning? Suppose you want to make a cake and have very little cooking experience. You read all about it in magazines, you study a few recipes, and then think you're good to go. You start following a recipe and realize you don't know what it means to "fold," "blend," "whip," or "test for moisture." All you've done is memorize a set of steps with no ability to put them into action or figure out what to do when something isn't written down or an ingredient is missing.

> "My students can get the right answer but they do not understand what it means."

Understanding how to bake a cake means knowing under what conditions and how you can alter the recipe, what all the terms mean, and how to make a judgment about quality on your own. Cake baking assumes a fair amount of prior knowledge about cooking, the nature of various ingredients, and the environments within which you are cooking. Would peach jam be a good substitute for extract of vanilla? If you stick a toothpick into the cake and it comes out dripping with ingredients, is it done? What if . . . ? Suppose . . . ? Our ability to answer hypothetical questions like these often reveals the depth of our understanding. I eat more cakes than I bake, so I hope this makes sense!

It works the same with subjects in school. For example, if you are studying local, state, and federal government in Grade 3, we want you to be able to do more than memorize the names of people in office. We want you to be able to read about what governments do and tell us about a local issue and how government can help solve it. We want you to create a class government patterned after a local or state government and be able to work to solve real problems as they do in the state capitol. (This, by the way, is one way some educators like John Dewey saw education as a life experience, and not preparation for life.)

We want you to be able to compare state and federal government, explain the similarities and differences, and tell us what a president can do in a given situation. In other words, understanding about government means far more than memorizing a list of names or rules. It means being able to use the information in different contexts. This is part of what we mean by taking action or applying what we have learned in an inquiry unit using a strategy like KWHLAQ.

Figure 7.1 is a list of intellectual tasks, in order of increasing challenge, that we hope students can perform to demonstrate their understanding:

We will, of course, use such a list as it relates to the abilities of our students. I share the entire list with you to suggest a full array of intellectual tasks from which to choose as we construct our summative assessments. We might use any one or more of these in order to determine the depth and quality of our students' understandings of what we've been studying. It is not sufficient to memorize information, store it, and repeat it back. This is no way to learn for understanding, and it does not foster the ability to use such knowledge now or in the future. We know from research (e.g., Mayer, 1989) that students must think constructively about information if we want them to be able to use and apply it at a later date.

For example, when Liz Debrey of Whittier International Elementary School in Minneapolis wanted to determine the depth to which her fourth and fifth graders understood the basic cultural elements of their study of ancient civilizations (Greek, Roman, Egyptian), she and her colleagues challenged their students to **compare and contrast elements** of ancient cultures with what exists today in three specific areas and **draw reasonable conclusions**. And returning to Carol Cutrupi's oceans unit (Chapter 4), we can see how she determined the quality of students' understanding of dependence and interdependence by how they solved the problem of their species' potential extinction. We will examine more specific assessment experiences next.

Fig 7.1 List of Intellectual Tasks

- Define *(e.g., Democracy is a form of government.)*
- Explain *(e.g., Give reasons for how democratic governments function.)*
- Exemplify *(e.g., Present examples of one or more democracies.)*
- Compare and contrast *(e.g., Compare and contrast democratic governments with each other and with totalitarian and fascist regimes.)*
- Draw conclusions *(e.g., Draw conclusions about comparisons and differences between democratic governments and totalitarian and fascist regimes.)*
- Identify and analyze problematic situations *(e.g., Identify the conflict between rights of the individual and society at large.)*
- Apply *(e.g., Apply the concept of democracy to any emerging government in another area, such as Latin America, Africa, or Asia; analyze the strengths of these emerging governments in accordance with the characteristics of a democracy and draw your own conclusions.)*
- Generalize from different examples and data *(Make generalizations about democratically elected governments based upon the experiences with different states, nations or countries.)*
- Create models, metaphors, and analogies *(e.g., Create a model government in a new country, a model of photosynthesis, or an analogy for plate tectonics.)*
- Hypothesize *(e.g., What would happen if certain conditions were to prevail within our own (or others') democracy, for example, censorship of the press, curtailment of the right to freedom of assembly, growing intolerance for those who are different, and so on?)*
- Generate or respond to questions *(e.g., What if generals of the army made foreign policy?)*
- Teach the concept *(e.g., Teach the concept of democracy to children in elementary school, using examples from the their own lives.)*

Giving Students a Choice

I think by now we can all agree that when students have choices to make from a variety of alternatives, they are more likely to be involved in any project. Just recall your own school projects; perhaps a teacher assigned you to learn about the exports of Peru, or said, "Pick any country in South America; find an area of its industry or culture you like, learn about it, and find ways to tell us what you've learned so that we want to visit the country." Having choices is empowering and leads to our sense of agency or control over own lives (McCombs, 1991). Having choices is one way to help students reach their own goals for learning and self-actualization (Marzano, 2003, p. 148).

If we are advocates of "child-centered learning," then we will recognize that affording students opportunities to make choices about content, approaches, and assessments is a key element of this approach. If you are a believer in the efficacy of tapping into students' varied "learning styles" (or to use Gardner's term "multiple intelligences"), then you will see the efficacy of affording students choices in how they learn and share their knowledge. And if you believe that students' interest can play a role in fostering learning, then you will afford them opportunities to make choices about what to learn and how to share their understandings. I certainly can attest to the latter in my *Othello* unit when we had students writing poetry and music and drawing cartoons.

And if you are a more "traditional" educator who makes most or all decisions in a teacher-directed unit (see Chapter 5), you can begin to experiment with choices in assessments—give students opportunities to make decisions about using different formats for their reports, their projects, and their summative assessments. Here is an easy way to begin experimenting with students' choice, one that is sure to reap rich rewards. I remember the high school science class where in May the teacher gave his students the choice of any of the remaining half-dozen chapters to learn and report on in any way they wanted. The best I saw was a video explaining the nature and actions of tornadoes presented by two special education students. They didn't like sitting in rows, listening, taking notes, and being so passive all the time. As one said, "We like doing stuff, working with our hands." I wouldn't have known that these students had any special needs were there not teacher aids in that class over time whose responsibilities included ensuring that they understood the content.

Knowing About Assessment at the Beginning of a Unit

All we have to do is reflect on my experiences mentioned previously, designing a test the night before administering it, to realize that students are better off knowing in advance what they are responsible for. If we craft an excellent problematic scenario to engage students' thinking and feeling, we will have provided a good structure for an entire inquiry unit. (See once again Carol's oceans scenario in Chapter 4.) We can argue this case from the standpoint of fairness. Students deserve to know in advance what they will be assessed on because it is fair.

We can make this case can from the point of view of instructional organization. When students know their responsibilities in advance, we and they have created a good structure for their learning. Less haphazard material is thrown in just for good measure. And we can argue that organization is the best kind of motivator. "I know what direction I'm going in; therefore, I can better prepare myself if I think this learning is important."

Remember the words of John Dewey quoted in Chapter 2: "A question to be answered, an ambiguity to be resolved, sets up an end and holds the current of ideas to a definite channel." The question drives the investigation and sets the structure for inquiry. We violate this principle so often that it may seem odd to champion designing units wherein students know from the beginning what they're going to do at the end. However, it makes sense from many perspectives.

Authentic Assessments

Grant Wiggins first brought the concept of authentic assessments to mind. Let me cite his criteria:

a. Problem-based tasks are "authentic" if they are realistic, relate to what we do in the world—e.g., solve problems, make decisions, hypothesize, experiment, and create

b. Require judgment, innovation and use of knowledge and skill.

c. Ask students to "do" the subject.

d. Replicate contexts in which adults are "tested" in the workplace, civic, and personal life.

e. Allow appropriate opportunities to rehearse, practice, consult resources, and get feedback on and refine performances and products. (Wiggins, 1998)

These criteria are important because they relate directly to what we've said about using and applying knowledge by challenging students at Levels II and III of the Three Story Intellect. It is also in accord with research by Mayer (1989) and others (Marzano, 2003) that we need to actively think about information and concepts in order to retain and be able to use them. So assessments that do more than ask students to repeat knowledge stand a better chance of positively affecting achievement as well as transferring knowledge to novel contexts.

DESIGNING RUBRICS FOR ASSESSMENTS

One of the aspects of assessment that has always bothered me is to hear of students receiving a paper or project with a grade on it and no explanation whatsoever. How crushing this can be for a child or a young adult to receive, for example, a C on their work and have no description by the teacher about why this was a C and not an A. An example of this comes from Madeline Swaney of Greensboro, North Carolina. She had spent hours writing a short story based on her love of science fiction:

> I knew the teacher would love the story, read it to the class, and give me the coveted A! The fever of that writing experience is still warm in my heart. The day finally arrived when the stories were returned. My hand trembled and my heart pounded as I reached for my paper. It continued to tremble as I realized what a fool I'd been. I was ashamed and embarrassed. MY paper, that had been so alive to me a few nights before, lay bleeding to death in my hands. The wounds on every line supported the C– in the margin. The intense pain of the grade would have been more easy to bear, if only some comment had been made about the story itself. Some word of encouragement or acknowledgment of my effort; but there was none. No words were written to me, the insecure, less-than-successful student, writer, human being! Communication about my paper wasn't to me, but to a machine that had mal-functioned on paragraphing, punctuation, and spelling—definite error in programming! (Barell, 1995, p. 95)

Fortunately, negative experiences can lead to positive growth and Madeline used that searing experience to become an English teacher who saw in every child "a valuable human being" who could create and soar beyond our expectations.

In teaching college, especially working with young people who wanted to become educators, we always worked out a set of standards with which we judged their work. So, in responding to a project, I would make a judgment based on these standards and then make specific suggestions about what needed to be done in order for this work to become outstanding. Some teachers later told me that they'd never received anything but an A on their work, but because there were comments related to our standards, they went ahead and modified their project to achieve the highest grade.

This is one reason for creating rubrics with our students—for all to know what we value and what we will be looking for in the final projects. How do we go about establishing a set of standards or criteria?

Here's one way to proceed:

1. Students at first will have difficulty identifying standards or criteria for excellence since they've never done this before. We might model the process by asking, "What makes a perfect birthday present?" Then let students discuss the criteria for such a gift: something you want, can use, is neat, no one else/everyone else has, and so forth.

   Ask them what makes a good movie. Identify the criteria they use to judge a good movie or their favorite TV show. Here, by the way, we will be working with my former colleague Matt Lipman's (1988) definition of critical thinking as making judgments that are based on criteria, or reasons, or what some would call standards.

2. Then move on to their projects. Ask students to think about their final projects and the quality of work we expect. "We all want to do outstanding work."

3. Ask, "What do you think an outstanding project looks like? Let's identify the reasons/elements/factors/characteristics/ that we all agree will make this outstanding. For example, we want our work to be written well—using good language, complete sentences, accurate spelling . . ."

4. "What else will your project have that demonstrates/shows us that you have learned and understand the topic?"

5. Once we have a list of standards/criteria, then we can ask, "What does each of these look like if we judge the project to be outstanding?"

   For example, if we say that you should know and understand the subject—What does that mean if we have a scale from 1 (doesn't know and understand) to 5 (knows and understands subject very well). Here we want students to help us think through what characterizes a 4/5 outstanding in terms of knowing/understanding content. Some other criteria might include presentation (oral speech; quality of art work); appearance of books/reports; mechanics (writing); organization; process of inquiry/quality of thinking; others?

6. List the characteristics that make a project a 5. For example, knowing and understanding content:

   a. Identifies important facts/information.

   b. Compares/contrasts these facts with others.

   c. Explain why they are important and draw conclusions.

   d. Answer questions from other students about topic.

   e. Answer "what if?" questions about the report.

   f. Other? (See Figure 7.1)

This is one way to proceed. Other ways involve showing students models of scoring rubrics we have developed, explaining their purpose, and asking students to modify and/or develop their own rubrics.

Here are some rubrics created by various teachers:

How the World Works—Legacies of Ancient Civilizations

Liz Debrey's used her rubric to help students self-assess their progress toward completing their ancient civilizations unit.

Here's the problematic scenario Liz and her colleagues worked on at several stages during the unit:

> You are an anthropologist who has been asked to write an article about your recent trip back in time to an ancient civilization. The article should be about how cultural concepts found in ancient civilizations have links to the modern world. In your article, tell which ancient civilization you investigated and why. Also, include at least three similarities between aspects of three cultures then and now. Finally, explain why your findings are important for people in today's world. Why do you think some aspects of culture have remained the same for so long?

RUBRIC FOR SUMMATIVE ASSESSMENT

Knowledge/Understanding of Topic

Includes three similarities from three cultural concepts linking ancient times to modern times.

| 1 | 3 | 5 |

Similarities are explained in detail.

| 1 | 3 | 5 |

Includes statement of why these similarities are important for us today.

1   3   5

Mechanics and Writing Style

Handwriting is neat.

1   3   5

Sentences are complete (caps and periods).

1   3   5

Article makes sense. It is understandable to the reader.

1   3   5

Five paragraphs are included 1. Introduction 2, 3, and 4 are the similarities and 5 states why these similarities are important for us today.

1   3   5

Scoring Criteria for Content Rubric

1 = Student includes one comparison from one or two cultural concepts.

3 = Student includes two comparisons from two cultural concepts.

5 = Student includes three comparisons from three cultural concepts.

1 = Similarities are explained with no details just listed.

3 = Similarities are explained with some details and some just listed.

5 = Three similarities are listed in each cultural concepts and explained in detail.

1 = Student includes one reason as to why these similarities are important today.

3 = Student includes two reasons as to why these similarities are important today.

5 = Student includes three reasons as to why these similarities are important today.

[Drawing their own conclusions with supportive reasons]

Scoring Criteria for Mechanics

1 = Handwriting is only barely legible throughout the article.

3 = Handwriting is somewhat neat throughout the article.

5 = Handwriting is neat and legible throughout the article.

1 = Only a few complete sentences are complete.

3 = Some of the sentences are complete.

5 = Most or all of the sentences are complete.

1 = Few of the paragraphs make sense.

3 = Some of the paragraphs make sense.

5 = Most of the article makes sense.

1 = Student includes one or two paragraphs.

3 = Student includes three or four paragraphs.

5 = Student includes five paragraphs.

As you can see, Liz has identified the scoring criteria/standards and then elaborated more fully on what she and students could look at in her "Scoring Criteria." In e-mail discussions while she developed these, we modified the above rubric and Scoring Criteria by adding, searching for, and analyzing differences as well as similarities. We felt that this was important because students could learn as much, if not more, from their analysis of why cultural elements were no longer manifest as from their examination of those that were still part of our lives. For example, we should ask, "Why don't we build buildings like the Parthenon and the Coliseum any longer?" We only use aspects or elements of these magnificent structures today. However, we do build magnificent sports arenas out of different materials, and sometimes we tear them down after thirty years of use. Why? I wonder.

This was the unit where we explored various ways to help students draw their own conclusions after making such comparisons and contrasts. Liz experimented with a number of different ways to help students go beyond the simple comparison and contrast exercise to the more challenging task of figuring out what it all might mean—to them, to the development of civilizations, to the arts involved, and so forth. This was not easy for some students until Liz introduced various stems—"What all of this means to me . . . This is important for architecture because . . ."

See Resource A for some of Liz's students' essays and for another challenging rubric created for questions in science that are "researchable."

CONCLUSION

Assessment is a vital part of our efforts because it is how we determine the degree to which students understand the topics they've been studying. As we mentioned, there are many different ways to determine what students are learning and we should use as many as possible as often as we can.

One question we haven't undertaken: "How do we know our students are improving in asking questions?" we must leave to another occasion. Just let me suggest here that this is an important question, and that one way to determine how our students are growing in their ability to ask good questions is for them to use their Inquiry Journals for every inquiry unit they engage in. If students are writing down their assignments, their curiosities, what they are finding out, and their new questions and conclusions about what they are learning, then, as Jill Levine, principal of the Normal Park Museum Magnet School in Chattanooga, Tennessee has discovered, students can easily reflect on their questioning and what they have done about it at the end of every unit, at the end of every year, and at the end of their time with us. Their reflections should be most interesting to them, to their parents, and to us. These reflections should propel them into the higher grades with a good deal of self-confidence.

RESOURCE A: STUDENT ESSAYS

Here are a few of Liz's students' final project essays. She and her colleagues have three classes of Grades 4 and 5 combined. How would you assess them? What can you tell from these essays and their conclusions about students' abilities to abstract, to think beyond the concrete and immediate?

12-20-06

Dear Reader,

I just came back from Ancient Rome. I discovered new things there. Now I will tell you about what I discovered. I studied daily life, traditions, and education.

First, I will tell you about daily life. Did you know that poor people lived in apartments and rich people lived in big houses? Today poor people live in the street and they work hard. In Rome poor people had to work hard, and when they got money it was for trading.

Now I will tell you about Rome's holidays and traditions, and then I'll tell you about today. In Rome when it was Valentine's Day, a boy would pick a girl's name from a hat, and whoever it was meant to be his girl friend for the year. Today on Valentine's Day we give cards and chocolate to girls and people we like or love. The Romans celebrated the New year on Jan. 1 just like we do. They also had fireworks at parties like we do on July 4th. Did you learn something?

Now I will tell you about education in Rome first. Did you know the girls did not have to go to school while the boys learned to write and speak better? Their pencils and pens looked weird and different than ours do today. In Rome they didn't write on paper. Did you know that many of the best teachers were slaves? Rome had many libraries. Now I will tell you about today. Girls have to go to schools. Teachers are not slaves. We write with paper and pens that are not strange, and we have many libraries too.

This is important because I learned a lot about ancient Rome and today.

Sincerely,

Manuel | Grade 4

Whittier International Elementary School

Minneapolis, Minnesota

12-20-06

Dear Reader,

I just got back from ancient Greece. There are many things that I studied. Leisure, daily life, and the arts.

Leisure: The Olympics were the same as they are today. Some games were different, but a lot are the same as today like the track and field events.

The Arts: They had paintings and statues as we do today.

Daily Life: The kids played with toys and we play with toys too.

This is important because I learned a lot about the past.

Sincerely,

Jacari | Grade 4

Dear Readers,

I just got back from traveling to the ancient Aztec civilization where there are lots of fun similarities to today's civilization. I was studying ancient traditions, arts, and fashion. I felt excited to compare another culture to mine!

I started off studying traditions. We have great similarities such as doing offerings at church. We also use temples for praying. Just like they did. At many weddings in ancient times commoners only had one wife just as modern times now.

I also had fun studying ancient art. Here are some of the similarities. We play harps just like they did. In ancient Aztec they also had festivals as well as we do now. We have Kwanzaa festivals. They had poetry just like we tell stories and write poems.

I ended my trip studying fashion. These are my final comparisons. Ladies now wear dresses like they wore in ancient Aztec times. We also both wear sandals. My last similarity is we both wear makeup.

This is important to me because there are less differences than similarities in ancient Aztec and modern days.

Shawnna | Grade 4

Dear Readers,

I can't wait to tell you what happened on my trip to ancient Egypt. I studied arts, leisure, and traditions.

Ancient Egyptian tombs were surprising because when a pharaoh died they had special tombs that were specially made, and decorated with a paint-like substance. This reminded me of the Lincoln Memorial. This was a special place to remember President Lincoln. Next I went to school. There were no girls. I asked where all the girls were, and they said that the girls were working at home. This reminded me of when girls and women had no rights. Then I went to see how their churches looked. I found one and it looked so similar to our churches today.

I then went to the Nile River to kill hippos. (It was a game). That reminded me of hunting sharks or whales. Then I went to the restaurant. Girls were dancing. That reminded me of watching T.V. and eating dinner at the same time. Then I saw a pharaoh watching a girls dance at a restaurant, and that reminded me of going to restaurants today that you can dance at.

Egyptian art was beautiful. They used curtains on windows like we do today. The sphinx reminded me of the Statue of Liberty because they are both pieces of art with faces of someone on them.

> *This is important information because architects can get
> ideas from ancient times. For instance, even though I did not
> study ancient Rome, I know that architects got the idea for the
> Metrodome from the Roman Coliseum. So, architects can get new
> and different ideas from the ancient ideas.*
>
> *Sincerely,*
>
> *Hassan*

RESOURCE B: OTHER RUBRICS AND FINAL PRODUCTS:

Sherezada visited the American Museum of Natural History during one
of our conferences on inquiry-based instruction. During her session,
she shared the rubric (on the following page) she and her New York City
sixth graders had developed for questions in science that were worthy of
purposeful investigations.

Asking "Interesting" Experiment Questions

Category	Excels (3)	(2)	Needs Improvement (1)
Type of Question	A question that compares variables. May start with "how does . . . ?" *Ex. How does [the independent variable] affect the [dependent variable] . . . ?*	A question that can only be answered by a "yes" or "no." *Ex. Does a plant move?*	A question that can only be answered by an expert. (May start with, "Why . . . ?") *Ex. Why is the sky blue?*
Vocabulary	Excellent use of scientific vocabulary. Demonstrates full understanding of words being used.	Use some scientific vocabulary. Does not demonstrate full understanding of words being used.	Does not use scientific vocabulary; instead uses pronouns like "it & them." If it uses some, does not demonstrate understanding of vocabulary.
Detail	Questions identify specific variables being investigated. Includes a detailed description of how the experiment will be carried out and what group will be measuring or looking for in the experiment. *Ex: How does the amount of water sprayed on the plant's soil every day affect the plant's speed of growth?*	Question identifies the specific variables being investigated. *Ex. How does the amount of water affect the plant's growth?*	Question gives a general idea of the variables in the experiment, but not the specifics of the variables being investigated. *(Look at identifying variables rubric for correct way of expressing variables.)* *Ex. How does the water affect the plant?*
Spelling/ Grammar	No spelling mistakes. Correct grammar.	One or more spelling mistakes. Some grammatical mistakes.	A lot of spelling mistakes. Incorrect grammar.

PRACTICAL OPPORTUNITIES

1. Select a unit you have completed. Redesign the formative and/or summative assessments for this unit, using the alternative, authentic formats just suggested.

2. For this unit be sure to emphasize challenging students to demonstrate their understandings of major concepts in various ways.

3. In what ways might you have introduced choice in this unit?

4. Repeat items one to three for a unit you are planning. Follow the planning processes outlined in Chapter 4 and identify problematic scenarios, objectives, strategies, and final assessments.

5. Be sure the summative assessments includes alternative formats, Levels II and III intellectual challenges and is authentic as previously defined by Wiggins (1998).

Art, Music, and Physical Education

"WHY DID DIEGO RIVERA'S PAINTINGS SHOCK THE WORLD?"

Arryon asked this question in his third-grade classroom as we were discussing people who make a difference in our lives—history makers. On that day, the students were considering artists and I presented them with this problematic scenario:

> Suppose you were asked to design a special wing for a Minneapolis art museum. In this wing, you wanted to place those people who have made a difference in our lives and the lives of others. Whom would you select, why, and how would you organize the exhibit?

This situation led to students' identifying many of their favorite artists as well as others they considered "heroes," such as Martin Luther King, Muhammad Ali, and Michael Jordan. Here in a regular classroom we were discussing the works of various leaders, heroes, and artists who had made major contributions to our lives, and the teacher, Linda, had obviously done an excellent job of introducing students to a wide variety of influential people. Students had other questions such as, "Who was the first artist?" and "Who invented electricity?"

From these initial questions, we identified the criteria students would use to select history makers to include in the museum exhibit; elements such as fame, impact on the world, and so forth. What was interesting about Arryon's question was that it immediately led to our working to have him and his classmates generalize the question. "How can we ask this question so it relates to all artists? To all of our special people?" Students struggled with this a little bit, but eventually they were able to ask, "What effect did these artists have on their culture and on other artists?"

Challenging students to ask broader, deeper questions is a task we engage in from the beginning of most units, because as so many of us find out, their original questions (like ours) are often at Level I or are somewhat limited. (See Liz's questions in the ancient civilizations unit, Chapter 6.)

Here is an example of how one teacher had made sure to include renowned artists within her unit on history makers. Too often we forget that artists are persons who help us look at our world from different points of view. Consider the abstractness and realism in Greek and Roman statuary; the anthropomorphism of Michelangelo's "The Creation of Adam"; the variations of light and shade in Monet "Haystacks" and in "Houses of Parliament" paintings; the purity of a Mozart concerto (e.g., for flute); the dramatic opening measures of Beethoven's Third, Fifth, and Seventh Symphonies and the jarring portrait of "Guernica" by Picasso. All of these artists have brought to us their varied visions of the world, some heavenly, some shocking.

And this is what a work of art is to me, not something that is "beautiful," although it very well might meet that standard. A work of art is an expression of how one person confronts and perceives his or her experience. Very often what results is a view of the world that is very different, from an original point of view (Consider Picasso's many color periods (e.g., his "Blue period") as well as his use of cubism (e.g., "Les Demoiselles d'Avignon"). A work of art challenges us to look at and experience life from the point of view of the artist and this often is shocking, as with cubism, illuminating, eye opening, comforting, and thrilling.

A work of art is one person's interpretation of experience. We may find any of the following in a work of art:

1. Expressions of deep feeling, as in "Starry Night," Chopin's Fanatasie in F minor, Op. 49, or in Chartre's Cathedral.

2. Varied points of view/perspectives/ways of seeing similar subjects—novel approaches to solving an aesthetic problem.

3. Examples of artists asking questions, such as "How can I represent this bunch of flowers or this landscape?"

4. Representations of the widest possible varieties of human and animal experience as in *Charlotte's Web*, *Franklin in the Dark*, and *The March of the Penguins.*

5. Representations of concepts and ideas through a widely varied array of media: music, painting, sculpture, weaving, dance, theater, architecture, and others.

6. A keen awakening of all our senses of perception.

7. Awareness of different historical and cultural eras and how works of art reflect same.

8. Aesthetic concepts such as uses of space, rhythm, rhyme, time, organization/composition, drama, color, texture, line, shape, and uses of language (e.g., simile, metaphor).

9. Specific skills required to create a work in any medium.

10. Examples of artists' use of creative, critical, and reflective thinking throughout the composing process. (Note how many times Beethoven changed the opening of his Fifth Symphony, whereas Mozart left his first draft stand as his final draft.)

> "Poetry lifts the veil from the hidden beauty of the world, and makes familiar objects be as if they were not familiar . . ."

In fashioning any unit we might bring to light any of these elements as we study and create art ourselves.

In *A Defense of Poetry* Shelly (1821) said, "Poetry lifts the veil from the hidden beauty of the world, and makes familiar objects be as if they were not familiar . . . [it] enlarges the circumference of the imagination by replenishing it with thoughts of ever new delight."

Sometimes we forget that an artist can bring to life that which is dimly perceived, only felt, or too abstract to understand. We have models of the atom, poems about love and sadness, pictures of great schools of learning (Raphael's "School of Athens"), and of terrible conflict (Delacroix, "Liberty Leading the People"). We have great monuments to the gods (Parthenon) and to vicious combat (the Coliseum).

Any unit of instruction can benefit by students studying the art of an era, the art that helps illustrate complex phenomena (think of plate tectonics, of the legislative process, and the act of creation itself).

As Shelly noted, poetry and, indeed, all of art, awakens us to see the familiar with new eyes, to behold and disclose what we have ignored or never seen, and to become aware of new realities amidst the conventional in our lives.

"I LIKE YOUR PAINTING BECAUSE . . . "

In another class, the art teacher had second graders draw various pictures of houses. Then we started a conversation about art. We asked ourselves, "What would two artists getting together talk about with regard to each other's art?" We generated a number of responses, but these are the ones we settled on for second graders:

- This is what I see in your painting.
- This is what I like.
- And here's what I'm wondering about . . .

During the class, students paired up and very quietly and somewhat tentatively began the process. We modeled it in the beginning and then the students were on their own. After about twenty minutes, we asked several volunteers to share what they saw and what they liked (a version of observe, think, and question) about their partner's drawing. From this process and these public sharings, we learned how some students used the various elements of art they'd been studying to create their own special views of the structures they were drawing.

Here, then, is a process that we can use as a formative or summative assessment of students' understanding of how to use form, color, line, texture, composition, and space. We wanted to help students become good inquirers about their own and others' works of art. It isn't enough for a teacher to say, "Oh, Juan I love that picture. You get an A!" We want our students to be able to critique their own work and say, "I like this because . . . " or "I need to work on this aspect because . . . " and to refer to some of the major concepts/skills and ideas in artistic creation we've been studying.

OBSERVE, THINK, AND QUESTION

Without realizing that I was modeling an inquiry process that I would later write about, I used this process of observe, think, and question when I was asked to visit several Introduction to Art History classes at Montclair State University. My favorite painting was Raphael's "The School of Athens." (For a good image of this painting, go to www.google/images.) Raphael painted this fresco in 1509–1510 in the Vatican's Stanza della Segnatura in Rome. As I worked with it, I began to see what others have seen therein, a visual image of the history of human thought. Here we have, at the center, at the "vanishing point" of three-dimensional perspective, Plato and Aristotle. Arrayed around them we have Socrates, Zeno, Epicurus, Diogenes, Ptolemy, Euclid, and Heraclites (in the image of Michelangelo). I asked students to tell me what they observed in the painting: "It looks like a school . . . they're working on stuff . . . conversing . . . studying deep subjects . . . it's all about reasoning . . . " and so forth.

What I found interesting and challenging was to follow up their observations with questions such as, "Where do you see that? What tells you that this is a "school," that "they're thinking," and that "it's all about reasoning." For in these statements we have students' tentative conclusions. Raphael may have set out to depict all of the above, but he used wide varieties of the human figure within a most ponderous setting (some think it reflects St. Peter's Cathedral in Rome under construction) with blue sky shining through to illustrate his "School of Athens."

Students observed people and their configurations, gestures, clothing, and physical placement in space. They then related these observations to their vast array of prior knowledge about people in various settings and then drew this conclusion: "It's all about thinking, reasoning, philosophy."

We can do the same with any appropriate paintings or other works of art with our students. Becoming good observers of art may help them become keen observers of nature and humanity. For example, consider how we could use the following pictures in one or more of our units of instruction:

- "Guernica," Pablo Picasso
- "Creation of Adam," Michelangelo
- "Mona Lisa," Leonardo da Vinci
- "School of Athens," Raphael
- Parthenon, Colosseum, and Pyramids (where we can examine the mathematics of these structures) in both Egypt and Central America
- "Haystacks," "Houses of Parliament," and "Water Lilies," Claude Monet
- "Voyage of Life," Thomas Cole (a set of four paintings depicting various stages of life; see also his "The Course of Empire")
- "Niagara Falls," Frederick Church (see also paintings of Andes, various brilliant sunsets and pictures of "Icebergs")
- "Snowstorm," J. M. W. Turner and other painters
- "Slaves," *Unfinished sculptures*, Michelangelo
- "The Thinker," and "The Hand of God," Auguste Rodin

- Figures in public spaces, Alberto Giacometti
- "Madame X," and "Roosevelt," John Singer Sargent
- "Girl with a Pearl Ear Ring," Johannes Vermeer
- "Oriental Poppies," Georgia O'Keefe
- "At the Theatre," Mary Cassatt
- "Self-Portrait," Frida Kahlo
- "In a Park," Berthe Morisot

And we could go on and on. For most artists, you will find excellent reproductions by going to www.google/images. Once again, our purposes here are severalfold:

1. To introduce students to the wonders of art.

2. Provide them with opportunities to see the world anew.

3. Give them practice in close observation of what artists have created.

4. Perhaps give them opportunities to think like an artist by reflecting on these kinds of questions: "How did he or she create this? Why did they do it that way? Make these choices? What were they thinking?"

5. Provide good, exciting pictures that supplement what we are studying.

For units in the various subjects, we can always find a variety of works of art to supplement our readings and to present a different point of view:

Social Studies	Literature	Science	Mathematics
Delacroix	Turner	Church	Pyramids
Manet, Monet	Coles		Parthenon
Cassatt, Kahlo			

It is important for us to consider works of art as creations reflecting one person's outlook on experience that may tell us a lot about their culture, history, science, and literature. Each artist opens up worlds of unexplored territories through his or her depictions of life within nature. Our arts are one vital, significant and, often, revolutionary way in which we make our worlds meaningful.

PARENTS AND ARTISTS

When my sister, Robin, was a young mother living in Wellesley, Massachusetts, she and a number of other parents participated in a volunteer program to bring art into the schools. One of the art teachers/supervisors thought it would be a good idea to bring them into the third- or fourth-grade classrooms in the several elementary schools and challenge students to become good observers of art. Robin received professional development experiences from the art staff and then on various occasions visited schools in Wellesley.

She remembers presenting the kids with two different paintings that might have challenged them to consider two works by the same artist or renditions of similar subjects by different artists. She doesn't now remember any specific artists, but her presentation made me think of the following possibilities:

Same Subject

Sailboats	"A Fair Wind" Winslow Homer and "The Long Leg" Edward Hopper
Children	"The Young Girls" Mary Cassatt and "Girl at Mirror" Norman Rockwell
Life in School	"Teacher's Birthday," Norman Rockwell and Raphael's "School of Athens" or Rembrandt's "The anatomy lesson of Dr. Tulp"
Life on a Farm	"Threshing Wheat" Thomas Hart Benton and "Fall Plowing" Grant Wood
Nighttime	"Starry Night" Vincent van Gogh and Hubble Space Telescope Images—thunderstorm, fireworks and Comet McNaught from Perth, Australia— (http://antwrp.gsfc.nasa.gov/apod/ap070205.html) and Milky Way over Utah (http://antwrp.gsfc.nasa.gov/apod/ap060801.html) accessed February, 2007

Same Artist—Different/Similar Subjects

- Claude Monet, "Haystacks, Houses of Parliament," and "Water Lilies" (Giverney)
- Pablo Picasso, heads, faces, and portraits
- Mary Cassatt, "The Young Girls" and "Breakfast in Bed"

- Frida Kahlo, two different self-portraits
- Michelangelo, "The Slaves" (unfinished sculptures) and "Pietà" (versions of this subject at different times in his life)
- Rembrandt, different self-portraits
- Any artist's different versions of the same song (e.g., Frank Sinatra's versions of "Night and Day," and John Coltrane's versions of "My Favorite Things")

What we can do with works of art is limited only by our own interest in the creative process, our willingness to spend a little time searching out images (here www.google/images is priceless!), and our creative ability to search for ways of making art part of every unit we undertake. Regardless of the subject, there is art work already created that can somehow enhance our perceptions of that topic and can further develop our students' abilities to become ever more acute observers, to reflect on these observations (tapping into prior knowledge), and to raise good questions about what fascinates them, like Arryon's question, "Why did Diego Rivera's paintings shock the world?"

It sounds very much as if I'm advocating using art as a medium to understand other subjects. This is one of our options. Another, of course, is to see art as various and widely diverse expressions of how we make meaning within the world—a subject of study for its own sake.

"If music be the food of love, play on . . ."

Of course, music in all its radiant manifestations is an art form and inquiry can be just as prevalent here as when working with the pictorial and physical arts (sculpture, architecture, pottery, and so forth). I grew up on classical music. My father was a concert violinist with the Minneapolis Youth Symphony Orchestra and there was opera in his family dating back to his parents' and grandparents' lives in Italy.

My wife, Nancy, has been a devotee of jazz and popular music since listening to "The Make Believe Ballroom" broadcast from New York City while she was a teenager living in Troy, New York. She has been a jazz DJ on a local National Public Radio Station and currently presents her own program "Jazz Spotlight on Sinatra" at http://www.live365.com/stations/nancyann3839. Needless to say, we have music playing in our house all the time, be it classical or "straight ahead jazz." So my reflections on music and inquiry come from deep roots although not a lot of experience in the classroom.

Here's what I'm wondering—

Can we introduce the wonders of music through students' observing, handling, and listening to the various instruments of the orchestra? This might be accompanied by Benjamin Britten's "Young Person's Guide to the Orchestra," or "Peter and the Wolf," or any other composition that showcases most of the instruments.

Can we introduce children to music through playing various pieces—jazz, classical, country, popular, hip-hop, ragtime, and so forth and then invite them to listen closely to give them practice in making observations about what they are hearing just as we do with a painting, a piece of "prancing poetry" (Dickinson), or a seashell?

For example, can we pique students' interests by playing the following in their entirety or in short segments depending on age?

- Maurice Ravel's "Bolero"
- Ludwig van Beethoven's Fifth Symphony
- John Philip Sousa "Stars and Stripes Forever"
- Billy Joel's "I'm in a New York Frame of Mind"
- Bruce Springsteen's "Born in the USA"
- Excerpts from *Dreamgirls*
- Miles Davis "Sketches of Spain" and "Kind of Blue"
- Charlie Parker with Strings
- John Coltrane's "My Favorite Things"
- Duke Ellington's "Take the A Train"
- Bill Evans "Trio at the Vanguard"
- Frederic Chopin's waltzes, scherzos, or polonaise
- Any good, clean hip-hop lyrics

You get the idea. What other musical selections would you select to introduce students to various styles of music? Would they be able to identify the various stylistic elements you wish to teach?

Can we introduce students to the wonders of classical music by using one or more of Leonard Bernstein's "Young Person's Concerts from Lincoln Center?" These videos, a little grainy but full of Bernstein's love of the music, depict his answers to questions such as "What does music mean?" "What is American music?" "What is orchestration?" "What is melody?" and "What is sonata form?" (available at http://www.kultur.com)

As I said previously, I haven't seen any of these ideas modeled in the classroom, but, obviously, to generate them I have drawn on my own experiences too long ago to recall, those of young teachers of music during their internships and from conversing with various art educators over the years.

Music—even more than the pictorial arts—can move us toward strong and positive emotions. I am still deeply moved by Mahler's Second, Tchaikovsky's Fifth, Beethoven's Seventh, and many other symphonies. The piano concertos of Tchaikovsky, Brahms, Schumann, and Grieg are unparalleled in terms of their power to create very strong melodies surrounded by full, luxuriant orchestrations. I could say the same about other orchestral pieces such as Vivaldi's and Glazanov's "The Four Seasons." And for sheer power, drama, and deeply moving melodic line nothing beats Puccini's "Nessun dorma" ("No one shall sleep.") from "Turandot."

Each of us will select music that is appropriate for kindergartners, first, second graders, and up. I do not pretend in any way to have any expertise in this area, only a deep and abiding passion for the music itself.

"WHAT'S MY GOAL AND HOW WILL I ACHIEVE IT?"

Physical education is an aspect of my schooling for which I have always felt very positively. I attribute my awareness of what constitutes good health, physical fitness, and agility to all of my teachers. In high school, I participated in gymnastics, played baseball, and ran cross-country and track. However, what I learned more than any specific skills was a general respect for keeping in shape through regular exercise and good diet. However, I've recently had two experiences in classrooms that relate to our focus on inquiry.

Goal Setting

One day at Elizabeth Hall International Elementary School in Minneapolis, I had the pleasure of working with a group of fourth graders. Their teacher, Todd Goggleye, had briefed me on their warm-up routines and the games they played. My goal was to model inquiry strategies, and it occurred to me in speaking with Todd that working on students' setting their own goals would be appropriate.

Todd put the kids through their warm-ups, including running, jumping jacks, stretches, and push-ups. As I got down on the floor, the young man in front of me blurted out, "You can't do push-ups!" I matched him and maybe even went one more. Then I got the basketball and took three shots from different positions around the key, making two out of three.

"How many did I make?" I asked the students sitting in their positions.

"TWO!"

"How many did I want to make?"

"THREE!"

"So, what's my goal?"

"To make three of three."

And then we were off on our exploration of how to set goals. Here were the two questions I wanted students to learn, use, and apply to their lives:

What's my goal?

How will I achieve it?

I asked them how to improve my own shooting skills—practice, practice, and more practice, they said. Then I asked them to identify some of their goals. At first, they spoke about goals in sports, but then we moved to goals in life:

I want to be a concert pianist.

I want to be a basketball player.

I want to graduate from college . . .

With each goal statement, I asked, "How will you accomplish your goal?" and heard from them variations on "work . . . study hard . . . learn from others . . ." and so forth.

After every other student volunteered his or her goal I would ask, "What are the two questions we ask ourselves if we want to be successful?" And they repeated in unison: "What's my goal and how will I achieve it?"

At the end of the class, I took the basketball again and approached the basket from three different locations and, most fortunately, made all three shots.

Why are these two questions important?

We know from Bob Marzano's (2003) excellent summary of *What Works in Schools* that one very important factor is goal setting: "Goals themselves lead not only to success but also to the effectiveness and cohesion of a team" (Schmoker, 1999, as cited in Marzano, 2003, p. 36). Other research points to the efficacy of our setting high expectations for all of our students. Beyond these studies of adults setting goals for others is the knowledge of the effectiveness of each of us setting goals for our own improvement, achievement, and success.

Barbara McCombs (1991) notes that setting goals for ourselves taps into our "inherent motivation to learn" (p. 6). As these fourth graders noted, their goals would be the spark that motivates them to work hard, study diligently, and wisely and monitor their progress toward achievement. Other studies suggest the efficacy of students' setting subgoals for their own achievement (Marzano, Pickering, & Pollock, 2001, p. 95).

One of the major findings from the business world is the efficacy of individuals and groups setting goals. "Research consistently has supported goal setting as a motivational technique. Setting performance goals increases individual, group and organizational performance" (Kreitner & Kinicki, 2001, p. 256). What we have learned is that "difficult goals lead to higher performance" and that for all goals what participants require is feedback—from others, teachers, students, and parents. We need to know how well we are working toward our goals and a self-scoring rubric can help a great deal toward this end (see Chapter 7). What I started in the physical education class, however, requires our follow-up in all of our classes.

REFLECTIVE PAUSE

How can we foster students' setting their own goals for academic achievement? Under what circumstances should we stress students' becoming more aware of their own responsibilities in taking control of their own learning? To what extent can our younger students participate in this quest for personal control?

Think back to Chapter 5 when we discussed a structuring set of questions for our students engaged in independent study:

Planning: What's my goal and how will I achieve it?

Monitoring: How well am I doing now?

Evaluating: How well did I do and what might I do differently next time and why?

What I'm wondering is under what circumstances we can model this process and encourage our students to follow it when working on projects or attempting to achieve specific academic goals.

"Let's create a game."

In Joe Wallraft's first-grade physical education class at Whittier International Elementary School in Minneapolis we did something different. Here we decided to create a game. Joe took several students aside and worked with them to create a game to play in front of the class.

What I did with the majority of the students was to discuss games, what they involve, how they work, and what the goal is. They knew a lot about games and had many favorites, some from class and some from the playground. We discussed sports on the national level seen on TV such as football, baseball, soccer, basketball, and others.

Our goal here was to encourage students to become good observers of what they see on the playing field and to become inquisitive about what they see and do not yet understand. So after a few minutes' preparation, Joe had his kids play a game that consisted of moving to and from the safe havens of the blue mats without being caught or tagged. It was a special version of tag with enough variations in terms of time, penalties, and so forth that observers had to figure out what was going on.

Students played the game for a few minutes, and then sat down and listened to and responded to their friends' questions:

"How do you play the game?"

"What are the rules?"

"What are the penalties?"

These were the Level I questions. Then they proceeded to Levels II and III questions:

"What happens if you forget the rules?" (Sounded as if it came from a child who had once done just that!)

And "How do you feel if you have to sit down?" (meaning, I think, that you've been tagged out)

In our debriefing one teacher said, "I like the process but not the sitting time." Here we discussed the issue of our priorities. When is the process of inquiry the content we are teaching? When is it appropriate in any class to take the time to focus on kids becoming good observers, analysts, questioners, and searchers for answers?

The tendency is to always be DOING, always on the go, whether it's running in gym, baking cakes in the kitchen, painting a picture, or building a model in physics or technology. When is there time to reflect on the process of inquiry? And how important is this process in all of our classes?

This class illustrates the issue of curricular priorities and our allocations of time in just about any class we teach. For example, if we want our students not only to have good physical skills, but also to be keen observers of how games are played and, perhaps more important, to observe how they manage their own physical, emotional, and intellectual lives, then we need to provide time to do what we did in Joe Wallraft's class—learn how to invent games and observe and question what we see.

One of the physical education teachers commented that perhaps he could spend more time sensitizing his students to ask questions about the best practices involved in playing certain sports (e.g., why we bend our knees before taking certain shots in basketball, why we spike in volleyball, why we use any strategy to win a game) what are the benefits and drawbacks of using these approaches? The point is to educate our students to do more than sit and take commands from an adult, but to sit up, identify situations that are perplexing, and ask good questions. Doesn't this goal apply equally in all arts as well as in physical education?

CONCLUSION

And in all of the classes we've discussed in this chapter one overriding lesson comes to the forefront: process is content. That is to say, that the inquiry process, learning how to become good observers and listeners, questioners, and critics is part of becoming an artist, part of being in control of what we do on the playing field. As one kindergarten teacher noted after a lesson on the senses: "What's important here is that they learn to ask good questions and not memorize stuff."

Process is content in all of our classes as well. If all we do is learn facts and do not have the opportunity to think about and question them productively, then we are not making our subjects as meaningful as possible (see Parker, 1969).

Process is content when we provide time for students within the KWHLAQ process to inquire as if they were young scientists, historians, explorers, novel writers, or mathematicians. "What do we want and need to know about this situation?" requires we think as professionals in the subject so we can tackle a wide range of complex, ambiguous, and difficult-to-understand situations in all our subjects.

Process as content is not a new way to think about what we teach, but is an essential one.

PRACTICAL OPPORTUNITIES

1. How could we have used artistic productions within any unit we have taught in the past?

2. In what ways might we encourage students to analyze and question works of art for a unit that we are planning for the future? What artists might shed light on our major topics and give us insight into history, culture, and people?

3. What are some of our favorite works of art and how might we share them with our students just to become more acquainted with what art is—products of the imagination that make the familiar unfamiliar as Shelly noted? Enter into your Inquiry Journal reflections on this favorite work of art.

4. What works of art do our students especially like—or their parents—and how can they share them with all classmates for observation, thinking, and inquiry?

"How Do We Involve Parents in Our Inquiries?"

"WHY DON'T YOU READ THIS BOOK?"

In the beginning are our parents and grandparents who first introduce us to the worlds we might eventually explore. In my case, it happened to be my maternal grandmother, Florence Wright Ferguson, who one day listened to the radio and happened on a broadcast of one of the first talk shows in media, hosted by Mary Margaret McBride. Her guest on this auspicious occasion was a navy man, a Rear Admiral, one Richard E. Byrd, to be exact. When she heard Mary Margaret interviewing Admiral Byrd, she must have known instantly who he was. In fact, she probably knew that he had claimed to be the first to fly over the North Pole, to have flown across the Atlantic directly after Lindbergh's historic solo flight (Byrd had two companions with him), to have flown over the South Pole, and by 1951 had led no fewer than four expeditions to Antarctica.

My grandmother listened intently because she knew that Admiral Byrd was the world's and this country's foremost living explorer of the polar regions. She might not have known about his predecessors—men like the Norwegian Roald Amundsen, the first at the South Pole in 1911; British explorer Captain Robert Falcon Scott, who arrived about a month later and died on his return with all four of his companions; and Sir Ernest Shackleton, whose ship *Endurance* was crushed in the Weddell Sea in 1915 precipitating one of the most harrowing survival tales in all history.

While visiting my home in Needham, Massachusetts, when I was in seventh grade, she told me about the broadcast and, since she knew I had to do a "book report," she recommended that I read a book by Admiral Byrd. I followed her suggestion and this led to an amazing story of inquiry, exploration, and adventure that continues to this day.

Not only did I read all of Byrd's books (*Alone*, *Little America*, and *Discovery*), but I also read the books of Scott describing his tragic last expedition. These led to reading about Amundsen and other explorers. My book reports for seventh and eighth grade were all on polar literature and I am, of course, thankful to these English teachers for their support.

I became so curious about the Antarctic and about Byrd's expeditions that with my mother's help I launched a letter writing campaign. I asked the pilot of the plane that flew over the pole about his experiences. I wanted to know from the second in command about sledging across the Ross Ice Shelf to explore the Queen Maud Mountains and I wrote to the secretary of the interior wondering if it were possible to buy a few acres of land at the base of Mt. Grace McKinley to the east of Byrd's base camp, Little America.

> "I became so curious about the Antarctic and about Byrd's expeditions that with my mother's help I launched a letter writing campaign."

And, eventually, with my mother's continued encouragement, I wrote to Byrd himself. To this day I retain in my archives the eight by fourteen yellow legal-size rough draft to Byrd with some corrections by my English teacher, Mrs. O'Leary. I sent it off and waited week after week after week without a reply. Figuring that the admiral was just too busy to care about a thirteen-year-old wanting to participate in his expeditions and learn as much about them as possible, I probably became resigned to the silence.

But one April day, with the daffodils in mother's garden bursting forth in full color, there came to 23 Webster Park a letter from the world's foremost polar explorer. Written in blue ink with an authentic signature on white bond paper, Byrd answered all my questions, saying in response to one about finding oil in Antarctica that he'd found enough coal to supply this country for many years and that he was certain there was also oil beneath the surface. "You are entirely right . . ." he said about the possibility of finding oil. Imagine the thrill of a thirteen year old receiving that confirmation.

These letters led not only to my meeting Admiral Byrd in person on two separate occasions and his inviting me to come exploring with him, but also to my joining the U.S. Navy, sailing to Antarctica on Byrd's flagship, *USS Glacier* AGB-4 (he had since died), and discovering just how powerful a dream can be.

In my case, pursuing this dream with full support of grandparents, parents, and teachers enabled me to explore Antarctica. Furthermore, exploring Antarctica became a model or metaphor for my work in education—that we are all explorers in search of new, challenging, and exciting territories to discover. One of our jobs as educators is to help students search for their own south poles, to help them when they fall into the crevasses of life, and to set their sights anew on these goals and tantalizing horizons (see Barell, 2007b).

As Robert Scott wrote in 1903 while exploring the polar plateau west of McMurdo Sound where his ship, *Discovery*, was frozen: "Before us lay the unknown. What fascination lies in that word."

REFLECTIVE PAUSE

Upon completing a brief overview of this story with a few pictures for teachers I ask them to reflect on those persons in their family or elsewhere who significantly contributed to their growing up as an inquisitive person. Who modeled inquisitiveness for you? How has this affected your life as an educator?

"DID YOU EVER WONDER . . . ?"

Have you ever noticed this fascinating phenomenon?

The sun at its zenith seems smaller than it does at the horizon.

My grandfather once asked me, "Johnny, have you ever wondered why the sun appears so much larger while setting on the horizon than it does at the zenith?" Because he had taught me, I knew what a "zenith" was.

"No, Granddaddy, I haven't," I responded as we gazed out his apartment building overlooking the Hudson River in New York, quite near the George Washington Bridge. From his window, he could see clear across the Palisades and off into New Jersey.

"Well, let's see if we can figure it out," and with that he led me to consider the dust in the atmosphere, what happens to light when it shines through this atmosphere, and eventually, I came to realize that light from the sun shining through the atmosphere as it sets (therefore there is more of it) will distort the image of the sun.

Llewellyn Ray Ferguson was a research chemist for General Foods, and in 1925 he received his first U.S. Patent for a gelatinous dessert using saccharine for diabetics known as D-Zerta. He was always asking me, "Johnny, did you ever wonder . . . ?" how we can tell the Earth is rotating on its axis, for example. And with that we trooped up to the Stamford, Connecticut, museum to see the pendulum swinging back and forth over a compass rose. The earth's rotation causes the pendulum's position to move around the rose inscribed on the floor.

REFLECTIVE PAUSE

What kinds of experiences do we have that cause us to wonder and to what extent do we share our wonderings with our children?

"I just don't believe it!"

Once, while she was in high school, my mother was watching the snow fall in her little town of LeRoy, which is between Buffalo and Rochester. Her father, the famous scientist who eventually won four patents for D-Zerta, joined her. "You know, Betty," he said quietly as they both gazed out the window at the falling snow, "the most amazing thing about the snow is that each of those flakes is unique."

Betty, a lover of language like her father, knew instantly what that meant—the snowflakes falling on her front lawn today with the prospect of no school tomorrow, each one completely different from the other.

"I don't believe it," she said.

"What do you mean 'I don't believe it'?" he said with some frustration. After all, he was the scientist and she was challenging his conclusion.

"I don't believe that they're all unique. That's all."

"Why?" he asked.

"Well, have you seen all of the snowflakes in the world?"

And with that L. Ray Ferguson (he didn't like to use his first name) stalked off probably muttering something about what they teach kids in schools these days. When escorting my mother around the American Museum of Natural History a few years ago, we entered the Hall of Planet Earth. I reminded her of this family story and she laughed and said, "And I don't believe all the grains of sand in the world—as many as all your stars—are unique either."

I said, "They are."

And what do you suppose she said?

"How do you know they're all unique? Have you seen/examined all grains of sand? How can you make such a sweeping generalization?"

REFLECTIVE PAUSE

What stories do you have that reflect on the inquisitiveness and critical thinking of those in your family?

"Ray, can you take the other side of the issue?"

My father had been a debater in college and wrote a humorous column for his junior college newspaper.

He loved to debate with my grandfather. I remember many occasions of sitting and listening to their debating the politics of the early 1950s and seem to recall their intellectual entanglements over FDR's New Deal. If you were a Republican, you probably saw it as social welfare or socialism at its worst. If you were a Democrat, you might have seen it as a form of governmental assistance during the Depression that created jobs and established our current social security system.

My mother tells the story of her dad and mine arguing over the New Deal with her father getting all wound up over the ills of the government's intrusion into our lives, spending all that tax money for job creation, and so forth.

My father would patiently listen and then ask, "Okay, Ray, can you take the other side of the issue?"

My grandfather would look at him in stunned silence and retort, "Why would I want to do a damned fool thing like that?" The idea of seeing both sides of an issue was too much for his ardent Republicanism.

REFLECTIVE PAUSE

How did you learn to be a critical thinker, one who needed to see evidence before drawing a conclusion, who challenged authority with sometimes impertinent questions, who could take both sides of an issue, who continually asked, "How do you know?"

THE AMAZING STORY OF THE WOLF SNAIL

When Sarah Campbell was just a little girl, she was out exploring with her parents and they found a skull beside the pathway. Encouraged by her mother and teachers, she and her classmates packaged it up and sent it to the Field Museum in Chicago to determine its nature. A scientist responded that he thought it had once belonged to a young collie. How did he know it was young? Because the bones hadn't yet fused.

When Sarah had children of her own and lived in Jackson, Mississippi, she similarly encouraged the curiosity of her young son, Nathan, who one day came bursting into the house saying, "Mama, mama, baby lions."

Sarah (personal communication) continues

> I went out and saw that he was pointing to two snails, which were crawling along one of the boys' Little Tikes trucks (the yellow plastic trucks). He indicated to me (I don't remember how now) that he wanted to bring them inside. I found a bucket and put some water in it because the snails were crawling along a wet surface. I had the notion that they were water snails, somehow. I brought the bucket upstairs and set it on the kitchen counter. I continued to get ready to go out. When I walked back into the kitchen to get something— a diaper bag or purse, the snails were crawling out over the edge of the bucket so I decided I needed something with a lid. I put the snails in a plastic lidded container.

> We went to the library to find out what we could about snails. We took the snails to school to visit Nathan's older brother's kindergarten class. We took lettuce to feed the snails. That year the snails died—probably of starvation.

With the help of Dr. Bob Jones, curator of invertebrates at the Mississippi Museum of Natural Science, Sarah and Nathan discovered that this was a "wolf snail," a carnivorous snail that preyed on other snails in the backyard. Evidently, what this snail does is move its head into the shell of another snail and retreat after having gulped the poor prey in one mouthful.

> Continued research led mother and child to another scientist, Dr. Melissa Harrington (Delaware State University), who had conducted research on wolf snails. In fact, to conduct her research, Dr. Harrington required a steady supply of these snails and offered to pay Nathan, now in first grade, $20 for each such snail.

> When we got to know Dr. Harrington via e-mail, Nathan became interested in what she was doing with snails. He also liked the idea of sending snails to her and getting $20 for his trouble. He wrote notes to her and drew her pictures, and last summer, when we drove up to Maine and New York State to visit friends and family, we stopped in Dover to visit Dr. Harrington and to see her lab. When Nathan was in first grade, he wrote to Dr. Harrington stating that if she ever grew tired of her lab, he would take it over for her.

In an article she wrote for *Highlights*, Sarah Campbell (2007) quoted Dr. Harrington:

> Wolf snails relate to prey snails in the same way that lions relate to zebras . . . they are bigger, faster, smarter, and rarer.
>
> In fact, when Nathan found his first wolf snails at the age of four, he ran into the house shouting, 'Mama, Mama, baby lions!' He did not know it then, but he had indeed found the lions of his backyard snail habitat. (p. 13)

> "In fact, when Nathan found his first wolf snails at the age of four, he ran into the house shouting, 'Mama, Mama, baby lions!'"

Had it not been for Sarah Campbell's own curiosity about the snails Nathan named Soldier and Ephenie "that crawled from his thumb to his elbow before he could say their names," this story would not have unfolded and Dr. Harrington's research on these amazing creatures would have slowed to a snail's crawl.

Jill Levine is principal of Normal Park Museum Magnet School in Chattanooga, Tennessee. She has fostered inquiry throughout her K–5 school in units that most often have a connection to one of the city's fine museums. But she is also a mom:

> As a principal, it is so gratifying to see students deeply involved in content learning. It often seems that our students are engaged at a level not normally expected of young children. As a parent of two young children, I have been able to experience this firsthand as my kindergarten son asks questions at the dinner table about what he has learned that day at school. When my son adopted a pet caterpillar, a teacher at school helped him call the butterfly expert at the aquarium to get advice on taking care of the caterpillar at each stage of his lifecycle. They then created a folder with important information. My son was so proud of this folder and it led to many discussions and questions. In this case, his learning did not take place while he sat at a desk, but the information learned will never be forgotten! (J. Levine, personal communication, 2007)

THE RABI FAMILY

Once upon a time at the turn of the twentieth century, a young father emigrated from Galicia, an area that is now southern Poland. He came to New York City and soon brought his family to live in the tenements of the lower east side. Eventually, father and mother Rabi moved over to Brooklyn not very far from where I once taught in East New York. Way back then this part of the city was probably still farm-land with cows chickens, and with roosters crowing at the break of day. (When I taught there at 7:20 in the morning, you could hear the rooster crowing—not the same one, of course!)

The Rabi's son, Isidore Isaac, soon filled their living room with all sorts of electronic gadgets having loads of fun experimenting with new technologies. Eventually, Isidore I. Rabi became a world-famous scientist working with Oppenheimer on the atomic bomb and on radar at MIT during World War II. He won the Nobel Prize in Physics for his pioneering work on the electron—investigating various properties.

Once, just before he died, a colleague asked him, "Why did you become a scientist, rather than a doctor or lawyer or businessman, like the other immigrant kids in your neighborhood?" His father had been a tailor and a grocery store owner in Brooklyn.

Rabi said, "My mother made me a scientist without ever intending it. Every other Jewish mother in Brooklyn would ask her child after school: 'So, did you

> "My mother made me a scientist without ever intending it. Every other Jewish mother in Brooklyn would ask her child after school: 'So, did you learn anything today?' But not my mother. She always asked me a different question. 'Izzy,' she would say, 'did you ask a good question today?'"

learn anything today?' But not my mother. She always asked me a different question. 'Izzy,' she would say, 'did you ask a good question today?' That difference—asking good questions—made me become a scientist" (Sheff, 1988, p. A26).

"That difference—asking good questions . . ." What a difference that would make at any level of instruction or professional development in the arts, in science, and especially in government! Imagine if we all, citizens and politicians, had been educated under Sheindel Rabi's loving care. Imagine the kinds of questions we would have asked in recent years about various domestic and foreign undertakings. It almost boggles the mind to contemplate where we might be today!

I have shared Sheindel Rabi's commitment to her children with hundreds of educators, and it never ceases to amaze me what this young woman who, according to her famous son, had not received the benefits of education beyond perhaps grammar school, understood about life, about learning, and about being successful.

"Did you ask a good question, today?"

Did *you* ask? Not, "Did the teacher ask and you came up with a good answer?" No, "Did you, 'Izzy,' pose a meaningful question? Did you sit up, take notice of something important, strange, and perplexing, and pose a question?"

Did you *ask*? Did you challenge the unknown, the authorities, the textbook, perhaps even the teacher, with a good question? Did you disturb the regular routine, did you challenge what we take for granted (as Keevan did with the title of this book), did you probe the mysteries of our universe by sitting up and saying, "I have a question!"

Did you ask a *good* question? Not just, "**Might I** be excused . . . **Can I** use the bathroom . . . **May I** borrow a pencil?" No, did you ask a "good" question? And, what is that? How do we define a "good" question? What are our criteria? (More later.)

Sheindel Rabi had no advanced degrees in pedagogy, curriculum, school organization, or brain mechanics. What she knew, however, from growing up in Galicia on a farm, I assume, was that those who ask the good questions are those who will not only survive, but who will prevail (as Faulkner famously said in his Nobel Prize address).

WONDER TALK

In a wonderfully enlightening book, Judith Wells Lindfors discusses children's inquiry and how it is used to make their world understandable. In so many informal contexts, Lindfors has recorded discussions between parents and children wherein they either seek information to make sense of some strange phenomenon or wonder aloud in a playful, more open-ended fashion.

For example, here's a brief excerpt from Jill and her mom's discussion about a book they are reading at bedtime:

Mother: (*reading*)	"But the red squirrel pushed and shoved him [the rabbit] until they were both settled snug and peaceful high up in the tree under the stars."
Jill:	Where do rabbits really sleep?
Mother:	In their holes.
Jill:	Under the ground?
Mother:	Uh huh. "The next day"—
Jill:	Do they have nest-es?
Mother:	They build nests in trees.
Jill:	Squirrels, too? (Lindfors, 1999, p. 1)

You can see how four-year-old Jill is attempting to figure out the difference between where squirrels sleep in this story and in reality.

As discussed earlier in this volume, Lindfors (1999) contrasts this information-seeking act of questioning with "wondering," where children are not asking formal questions but using language such as

> You know it's weird . . .
> There's a part I wanted to ask . . .
> I'm trying to figure out . . .
> This is what I don't get . . .
> I thought it was . . .
> I wonder why . . .
> Well, maybe . . . (p. 59)

You can see the difference. Jill is asking direct questions whereas another student might be openly speculating, trying to reason something out, or sharing a doubt or some perplexity. Information seeking is more closed ended—there are often correct answers. Wondering is more open, speculating on, and playing with possibilities. Wondering for Lindfors (1999) reflects the essence of play—an activity with intrinsic rewards, something we do for its own sake (p. 40).

We can engage in wondering by speculating on anything we are examining (e.g., seashells) or reading a book about the early colonists.

Not all inquiry is, in other words, expressed with who, what, where, when, and why questions with a teacher at the front of the room. We are often engaged in inquiry while driving to the park, examining a fish tank, reading a book, or just speculating on the size of the sun on the horizon and at its zenith.

REFLECTIVE PAUSE

How can we build on wonder talk?

How can we find time at home to engage with our children in observing what's interesting, perplexing, or fascinating and just play with wonderings as amusements that we might try to figure out at some point?

PARENTS IN SCHOOLS

When I used to conduct students through the various exhibits at the American Museum of Natural History here in New York City, I would always notice the parents who came as chaperones. Occasionally, some of the parents would engage me in discussions about the exhibits. On one occasion, I was standing in front of our actual T. rex fossil describing something about its age, or the regeneration of its teeth (an amazing characteristic and "How do we know?"), when I must have brought up the term "evolution" and something about religion, because a parent asked, "Which do you believe in, evolution or the religious interpretation?"

I said, "Both."

Parents were often engaged with their children about the various exhibits including the dinosaurs, the giant blue whale, or the long house of the North American Iroquois Indians.

In one school I worked with in Colorado, a first-grade teacher told me that when his students are engaged in an inquiry unit there are always parents involved—in his classroom or on a field trip. They become not merely chaperones but actively engaged participants. What better way to share with our parents what we are doing in our classrooms. Probably every school has a PTA or PTO. To what extent might they be involved in the inquiring lives of their students?

PARENT SURVEYS

Kelly Guzman is a second-grade teacher in Cherry Hill, New Jersey. During a recent unit on communities, she and her students created a parent survey to determine what it takes to create a successful, healthy community. As you learned from Chapter 4, Kelly and her colleagues were working with a problematic scenario wherein students were to learn about communities in order to figure out how to help New Orleans get back on its feet.

After helping her students learn how to interview parents, Kelly's students asked their parents these questions:

- *What are your basic needs for survival?* ("I need water, shelter, clothing, and food.")
- *What everyday needs do you have?* ("I need to eat and drink water every day. I need hygiene. I need to sleep in my bed or in a comfortable place.")
- *What are different ways to meet these needs?* ("I eat and cook healthy foods. I try to get plenty of rest. I practice hygiene every day. I get yearly checkups for my health.")
- *List some of the places in the community that help you meet your needs.* ("Shop Rite, Macy's, restaurants, doctors' offices (e.g., the eye doctor)"

In many other classrooms, teachers and students bring parents into the classroom by sending home surveys or what one Minneapolis teacher (at Earle Brown Elementary IB World School) called a "template." "Let's take the students' question and put them on a piece of paper—perhaps one per child—and send them home so students can get their parents' ideas about what they are studying." We know that parents want to be involved in their children's education, and these are quick and relatively easy ways of increasing the communications between home and school.

In Chapter 1, you read Robin Cayce's amazing story of her fifth graders interviewing members of the community who lived during World War II, and you may recall the amazing story of one parent/grandparent visiting her classroom with a captured Nazi flag, an experience no child in that room—nor adult—will ever forget!

REFLECTIVE PAUSE

In what other ways have we communicated our instructional priorities with parents? What are some other possibilities?

NEWSLETTERS AND SUCH . . .

We can communicate the essence of Sheindel Rabi's challenge to her son, "Did you ask a good question, today?," in many ways. A formal newsletter is one common way.

At the Edgewood Elementary School in Brooklyn Center, Minnesota, Principal Gretchen Peel sends out a monthly newsletter to parents with all sorts of news items: upcoming events, what students did in their classes on a particular day, special parent education opportunities, shopping deals with merchants, and notes about the changing seasons. With Ann Mock's able assistance, this is what Peel published in her February newsletter:

> February is a big month for migratory birds. Can you identify some of the birds landing in your backyard? Bird feeders are an excellent way to track migration patterns of birds. Next week, raccoons and skunks begin to wake up after their winter nap. When do you think the first raccoon will be seen? Spring is near! Now is a great time to prune apple trees and oak trees. (Peel, February 07, 2007, accessed March 21, 2007 at http://edgewood.district279.org/School_Newsletter.html)

Just look at the possibilities for parent-child inquiry in this newsletter:

> Let's go outside and see if can see some of the signs of February. Let's look for birds or raccoons or any animals. Let's become very good observers by asking ourselves, "What are they doing? How do different birds feed at this time of year—or any time of year?"

I am often amazed at watching how different birds—chickadees, sparrows, cardinals, and blue jays use the birdfeeder in our back yard. I wonder what accounts for these different behaviors—e.g., cardinals' flitting about from adjoining branch to branch several times before alighting on the feeder suspended about five feet above ground.

Also, "I wonder why it is best to prune these trees in very early spring? What happens if we don't prune them? What happens if we prune them in the dead of winter or summer?"

I can hear my grandfather openly speculating about so many of the facts in this marvelous newsletter from a school whose question in another newsletter is, "What's the Big IDEA?" IDEA is their acronym for Inquire, Discover, Explore, and Achieve.

In a newsletter, we could share students' questions from each class-room. For example, in Laura Karsjens' kindergarten class (Earle Brown, Brooklyn Center, Minnesota), they were studying the effects of light. Laura decided to give her students "the problem of taking light away [and that] would be an excellent way to make them more aware of light." This stimulated lots of thinking about our need for light to live and work. Around a large picture of a light bulb on the board, Laura wrote down all of their questions. This experience led a rather quiet boy named Logan to ask, "If the sun is made of gas [and light comes from the sun], is light also a gas?"

> "If the sun is made of gas [and light comes from the sun], is light also a gas?"
>
> —Student in Laura Karjens' kindergarten class, Brooklyn Center, Minnesota

This question caused me to stop and think for a while. We know that sunlight is a product of hydrogen's fusing into helium deep within the core of the sun. This fusion process results in the creation of helium atoms with a by-product of energy in the form of light photons explained by Einstein's formulation $E = mc^2$. (For an explanation visit http://observe.arc.nasa.gov/nasa/exhibits/stars/star_6.html.)

Laura and I corresponded about how her class could find answers. She received some good ideas from a high school physics teacher. I wondered what her students' parents might do with such a question. Perhaps we include some of these very challenging student questions in our newsletters to inform parents of how insightful and challenging their children are as well as to invite their participation in seeking answers.

Years ago, my colleague Art Costa used to tell of schools that used all their resources to communicate to parents about the importance of challenging students to think. He noted examples of using all of these means of communicating that high priority to parents:

- Newsletters
- Logos on stationery, pencils, T-shirts, calendars

- Notes home
- Mission, meetings, and priorities of PTO and PTA organizations

In other words, if we are really serious about challenging students to inquire, conduct purposeful investigations, think critically, and reflect, then we should use all of ways of communicating with folks at home.

PARENTS AS RESOURCES

Robin Cayce's fifth-grade unit in Chattanooga is a marvelous example of how parents and grandparents can be involved in their children's education. As we saw in Chapter 5 when we embark on a long-range inquiry approach that calls for students to identify what they know, what they want to know and how they will go about finding answers (KWHLAQ), we give students a golden opportunity to identify their parents as potential resources.

In working with fourth graders in a South Carolina classroom recently, we observed that one boy's father was in construction. This was most appropriate because the class was working in a unit on how geometry is used in architecture. What better person, perhaps than an architect himself, to explain why, when building a large structure, we must be very sure to have right angles where appropriate and why all surfaces must be level and plumb.

In a unit on religion with fourth and fifth graders, Liz Debrey at Whittier International School has called upon various professors, and men and women of the cloth to share their knowledge, stories, and questions about their areas of expertise with students.

How have you and your students accessed the resources at home to provide expert insight into some of the questions students have been asking?

EDUCATING OUR PARENTS

Sylvia Mathis has been a teacher in Salt Lake City for several years working with programs such as future problem solvers. Sylvia and I worked together with the Association for Supervision and Curriculum Development (ASCD) for many years during the push to enhance the degree of students' critical thinking in classrooms.

One thing I always marveled at with respect to Sylvia's school and how it operated was that whenever the teachers received professional development that challenged students to think, Sylvia and her colleagues and shared this experience with parents. They wanted parents to know what they knew. They wanted parents to continue the high levels of challenge experienced in the classroom at home.

CONCLUSION

All these stories illustrate what we all know growing up—our parents are our first and often our best models of how to live in the world. I learned to wonder about the natural world from my grandfather, to be skeptical from my mother, and to "Never, ever give up" from my father. Nathan Campbell learned all about the wolf snail because his mother and grandmother were very curious about the world and shared this passion for knowledge with their children. Isidore I. Rabi grew up to become a world-famous and Nobel Prize winning physicist who helped win World War II, because every day when he returned home from elementary school, his mother asked, "Izzy, did you ask a good question, today?"

One of our challenges as educators is to tap into the wonderings of our students' parents and to bring them into the classroom through a variety of direct and indirect means. Their support can help us along our various journeys of inquiry.

PRACTICAL OPPORTUNITIES

1. What have our parents modeled for us?

2. In what different ways do we encourage the parents of our students to join us in our journeys of inquiry?

3. How have students' parents contributed to helping students find answers to their questions?

4. How can we plan for parental participation in future inquiry-based units?

Inquiry and Students With Special Needs

"WE DON'T LEARN THAT WAY"

One of the most intriguing lessons I've ever learned from students is that not all of us learn in the same way. Two boys told me this after I'd seen their homemade video describing the terrible nature and effects of tornadoes.

In May, their teacher at Dumont High School, New Jersey, had challenged his students to select a chapter from the textbook to read, learn more about, and share what they thought was intriguing and important. These boys created the video because, as they told me afterward, "We don't learn that way." Which way? "Everybody sitting in their seats, listening, and writing. We like to work with our hands," one of them said. I knew while watching their video that these high school students had been described as students with special needs. I've forgotten what special needs they have, but I haven't lost the significance of their message: not all students can sit still, listen to someone else talking, and master the content in any subject in that fashion.

Here are some of the key elements in this little episode:

A. These students accepted a very high level of intellectual challenge from their science teacher, Herb.

B. They were encouraged to exercise as much control over their learning as possible—over the content, objectives, and ways of sharing their learnings.

C. With help from their teacher and support personnel, they found their own point of entry into weather, a very complex phenomenon, and worked within a carefully constructed structure—something they also helped create.

D. These high school students did not require more time than their peers, but some students do require additional time.

E. And they made the topic of tornadoes meaningful in their own special way.

I've always remembered this end-of-term project, because it illustrated several important concepts that are meaningful for all students:

- Access to **alternative** resources, learning, and assessment strategies.
- Having **shared decision-making control** over means of learning.
- Creating **structures for learning** that afford flexibility.
- Using and planning **time** effectively.
- Close **support** from experienced educators and parents.

THE UNDERLYING "I CAN AND SO CAN THEY"

Michelle Thoemke is a special education teacher at Elizabeth Hall International Elementary School in Minneapolis. During a three-day visit to her school, I sat down with the students in her classroom and found out what they were learning about the human body. Most students were in the second grade and there were about six students in the room on this day.

What I distinctly remember from this visit was one student who was kind of rolling around on the floor as he spoke. It reminded me of a description of the young scientist and Nobel laureate Richard Feynman—as a young student, he would sometimes find it necessary to act out his thinking:

A Cornell dormitory neighbor opened Feynman's door to find him rolling about on the floor beside his bed as he worked on a problem. When he was not rolling about, he was at least murmuring rhythmically or drumming with his fingertips.

For the scientist who served on the *Challenger* commission and who figured out that the explosion of this space shuttle had been caused by

O-rings that had been damaged by freezing temperatures, scientific thinking was "a process of putting oneself in nature: in an imagined beam of light, in a relativistic electron" (Gleick, 1992, p. 244).

So maybe the boy I saw rolling around on Michelle's rug that morning in September was a young scientist working out his ideas. And maybe the often annoying repetitive actions of some students—tapping their fingers, their feet—are ways they have of working out problems and issues. Maybe they are junior Feynmans!

Those who watched Richard Feynman "in moments of intense concentration came away with a strong . . . sense of the physicality of the process, as though his brain did not stop with the gray matter but extended through every muscle in his body" (Gleick, 1992, p. 244). For Feynman and perhaps for many of our students with special needs, thinking may be a very visual process. We know it was for Einstein who thought in "more or less clear images" (Ghiselin, 1955).

> "I decided that 'I' was the limiting factor in what my students could do. I kept saying, 'They can't . . .' but maybe what I was really saying was, 'I can't . . .'"

Michelle is very reflective about her teaching. In an e-mail she shared one of her personal journal entries:

> For the past 5 years, I have been trying to leave Special Ed. I have been working on other licenses and thinking about what else I could do with my life. This summer I decided that this year I was really going to focus on being good at what I do (*I decided that "I" was the limiting factor in what my students could do. I kept saying, "They can't . . ." but maybe what I was really saying was, "I can't . . ."*) [italics added] I decided that they CAN. I just have to figure out how to make it happen. And I knew it wasn't going to be easy, but I like challenges. (M. Thoemke, personal communication, October, 2006)

Michelle's message is one from which all teachers can learn. Sometimes we just say, "Oh, they can't do it because of [list here so many of the limiting factors: home environment, SES, previous educational experiences, psychological/physical factors] . . ."

But, sometimes we are the limiting factor ourselves. We create what poet William Blake in "London" called those "mind forg'd manacles" that constrain how we think about our own abilities and those of others. If we are to succeed with any students, we need to have Michelle's faith that they can learn and we need to find those alternative ways to make it happen.

ONCE AGAIN—PLANNING, MONITORING, AND EVALUATING

Earlier in this volume I mentioned helping students take more control of their own learning by engaging in a process of planning out their goals and figuring out how to reach them; closely monitoring their own progress, and engaging in self-assessment once the work has been completed.

I note here the work of a prominent disciple of B. F. Skinner, the famous Harvard psychologist and proponent of behavior modification. One of his avid students is Doug Greer, a professor of psychology at Teachers College, Columbia University. For many years, Greer has been interested in students with special needs, especially those with autism. Through a behavior modification approach, Greer says, "We've shown four to seven times more learning in our autistic kids over control or baseline measures . . . If we can do that, we can sure as heck do it with children without disabilities."

Using specific verbal, pictorial cues, Greer has been working to help students from poverty as well as those who are autistic to "listen, ask, name, seek attention, modify ideas, move from seeing something to saying it, and move from reading something to writing it . . ." A firm believer in rewarding appropriate behavior, Greer and his teachers often use tokens, cookies, and other objects to signal approval. Dr. Greer is also a firm believer in helping students learn to exercise more control over their own learning:

> We show kids how to monitor their own behavior, how to set goals for themselves and, ultimately, how to reinforce themselves for what they've achieved. The goal, by fourth grade or so, is to make them independent, accelerated learners—to give them control of learning, so that ultimately they become 'bad teacherproof.' (Levine, 2007, pp. 25–43)

Edwin Ellis (1993) has noted that such planning strategies are very important for students with learning disabilities. For example, when reading literature, "Perform Goal Setting (Clarify why you are analyzing the chapter. Identify a goal related to this reason) . . . Start with Questions (Questions to find out what kind of information to look for) . . ."

Another strategy is FLASH:

Focus on the topic

Look for familiar information

Activate prior knowledge and ask questions

See what's connected, search for relationships

Hypothesize (p. 363)

These strategies have been designed for adolescents and adults with learning disabilities. Would they, or a modification thereof, work with elementary school students with similar challenges? I imagine they would. For example, if we want our special needs students to make good observations of objects, think and relate these observations to prior knowledge, and then ask good questions could we use:

Observe

Think and relate

Question

Michelle Thoemke has a multiaged class of special needs students. She has used a version of OTQ called the OWL:

Observations

What do you wonder?

Link it to your life

Michelle wrote: "I used a poster-sized picture of dew drops on a blade of grass. It was a very simple picture but it yielded a very rich discussion. I didn't give them any information, I just asked what they noticed."

Their observations included:

- You can see through the raindrops.
- It is probably summer and rain got on the grass.
- It could be one of those poky things like on a cactus.
- The drops look like marbles.
- It could be a piece of paper with a rip in the middle.

Their wonderings included:

- I wonder if a bumblebee sucked the poison out of it. (The tip of the blade of grass was red and some of them thought it might be a flower)
- I wonder if it is water or bubbles.
- I wonder if it is wet.
- I wonder if it stings.
- I wonder if it is grass season. (he meant the time when grass grows, in the summer)
- I wonder if the water will dry up.
- I wonder if water always dries up.
- I wonder what it would be like if I were in the bubble.
- I wonder what it would be like if we could shrink the state of Minnesota into the bubble.

REFLECTIVE PAUSE

What does Michelle's use of the OWL approach suggest to you?

Michelle concluded her observations thusly:

> It definitely helps to have a picture. We will keep practicing with pictures this week. I like this OWL format because it is simple enough to appeal to them, and very flexible so I can use it throughout the day in multiple subjects. The kindergartners were able to generate questions just as easily as the second graders.

USING PROBLEMATIC SCENARIOS

Kerry Faber teaches a fourth-grade classroom in Edmonton, Alberta, entirely composed of students with special needs. Through many conversations, some in person while on a visit up north and many more through e-mail, I've come to realize just how powerful the model is that was first demonstrated to me by the high school students previously mentioned.

Kerry is a firm believer in moving away from worksheets that students fill out and turn in. Her children's parents aren't always as comfortable with this approach because they, like most of us, learned one way and Kerry is presenting her students with a much higher level of challenge. For example, here's her description of an authentic problem situation:

> I gave my students a problem to solve. I told them they were working for a large pizza company and they needed to design pizza boxes that would fit the different sizes of pizzas the company sold. They needed to make the base and sides but no lid was required. I showed them different sizes and shapes of pizza that I had premade. (K. Faber, personal communication, March, 2007)

Kerry describes most of her students as very visual students who need to SEE what they are asked to do. So she modeled the construction process with different sizes of pizza. Let Kerry describe the lesson herself:

> I physically demonstrated the need for these pizza boxes to FIT exactly for the pizza each child would choose to design a box for. I kept asking "why" questions until they could give me numerous "plausible" reasons. (I had to take the time to do this because if they couldn't SEE and discuss the importance of the size of the box in relation to the pizza, some of them wouldn't process that requirement and meet it.) Then I showed them grid paper that they could use (an accommodation for differentiation of instruction) to build the box. I reminded them of a similar math activity they had done earlier in the year to connect prior knowledge and

begin to help them picture some of the steps they would need to take. Then, because so many of my students struggle cognitively, I asked them to tell me what steps would need to be taken for them to be successful in solving this problem. As different ones told me ideas I continually paraphrased and questioned until we had a set of steps written on the board for them to follow. I had also drawn pictures to accompany the text. I reminded them that once they began I was no longer the teacher, but the project foreman who would come and just check on their progress. They would have to work together in their groups to solve their problems as they arose.

REFLECTIVE PAUSE

What elements of our framework (mentioned previously) do you see here?

Wherein has Kerry provided high challenge, structure, time, and alternatives to complete the task?

One of the elements Kerry mentions that I hadn't noticed until rereading this e-mail along with others I've received subsequently is the extent to which she creates a learning structure with her students. Like so many students (not just those with "special needs"), some of us work better within a solid structure of time and procedures. I had assumed before meeting Kerry that we the teachers would need to create this structure, this scaffolding framework. But notice how she elicits this from their prior knowledge, thereby eliciting students' input and ideas for the process. Students thus have more control over their own learning. She also provided strong visual cues and models for their success. But did all her students complete this task without struggle?

Far from it. Kerry continues,

> During this time the children worked away on their own, helping each other by talking through what they were doing. Then they came to the part where they had to build the sides of their boxes. This changed the box from a 2-D model to a 3-D. This is where most of them got stuck. After a short while I asked them to stop. I told them I saw lots of struggling, and because I wanted them to be successful, I was changing the task a little. I said that now they would be trainees. I explained that a knowledgeable employee trains trainees and then they are expected to complete the work on their own once shown. I told them I would walk through all of the steps on the board *but no longer talk—they had to watch to see what it looked like.* [italics added] I proceeded to do this. They

watched intently. You could have heard a pin drop in the room. Once done, I said, "Okay, go ahead." Now there were discussions in groups that sounded like "Now I get it. / So that's what that means! / I think we could do it this way. / No, that doesn't look right. Here let me show you."

Kerry was not only modeling for her students but also for her student teacher who hadn't understood why the step-by-step process was so important. Following the process just described, the student teacher exclaimed, "Now, I get it. Now I understand what you mean about their needing to SEE it." She called it an "A-hah" moment.

Another, more specific element in Kerry's story is how carefully she monitored students' understanding of the task. As she said, she saw lots of them "struggling." That's when she stepped in to help them outline the specific steps to create the pizza boxes (demonstrating same without words):

> It's important to check that students understand the material you are teaching. The best way to do this is to check their understanding before they start to practice a new skill . . . Many teachers do this by having students go through the steps they will use to solve a problem before they actually do the work. (Algozzine & Ysseldyke, 2006, p. 19)

As we've seen, Kerry carefully monitored students' progress through this complex construction project and knew when her students were "struggling." In *Teaching Students with Learning Disabilities*, authors Bob Algozzine and Jim Ysseldyke (2006) outline several ways to help students overcome challenges posed by learning disabilities:

1. Provide alternative assignments to help students compensate for academic weaknesses.

2. Help students focus on relevant aspects of assignments.

3. Use concrete examples and demonstrations when teaching new content.

4. Provide opportunities for students to progress at their own rates.

5. Modify assignments to help students compensate for academic weaknesses.

6. Provide more opportunities for practice than required by peers.

Algozzine and Ysseldyke mention others including, "Provide opportunities for self-monitoring" (p. 26).

As I entered these seven items I wondered, "What elements here would not benefit all students?" What Kerry has done is to provide us with an excellent example of what we can do to challenge our special students to think productively.

Another consideration is to reflect on what we mean by "alternative assignments." Kerry believes, as I do, that her students are up to engaging in authentic, problematic challenges like the pizza box construction. She knows that with appropriate structures, time, and support that her students can think through difficult situations and need not be relegated to doing what one student called "workbook pages," or worksheets.

And I'm not sure that some educators who work with students with special needs view what they do as compensating for "academic weaknesses." It seems to me that educators like Michelle and Kerry believe that their students can do just about anything—they can solve real problems with viable, often creative or insightful solutions.

For example, in one science class Kerry's student teacher, Heather, was demonstrating how to make color wheels that illustrated the principle that "all colors are in white light." This is her rendition of what was not working out too well:

> Before she could continue, one student jumped out of his seat, came up to her model, and said, "I think we could come up with a better way!" He and a number of other students spent the next ten minutes discussing and demonstrating the pros and cons of different potential models. The rest of the class watched attentively. Heather continually paraphrased what they were trying to explain so the problem solving could continue. In the end, their colour wheels looked much different from what Heather had planned and we had some very engaged students. The interesting thing is—the boys who did most of the talking are our biggest behavior challenges when they have to sit for any extended period of time and just "listen."

On this occasion, Kerry reminded her student teacher "that this happened as a result of consistent opportunities the children are given to shape their own learning in ways that are meaningful to them." (personal communication, March, 2007).

Shaping our own learning experiences requires teachers be willing to share some control over decision making with their students, and this means having a mindset that our students can be curious, creative, and very productive.

BUT CAN THEY ASK GOOD QUESTIONS?

We'll return to some of the outstanding work Kerry has shared with me momentarily. In response to this question, let me share with you another experience. I walked into a classroom of five special needs students and was asked to model the inquiry process and to challenge students to think mathematically. In this room seated around one of those neat semicircular tables where you can nicely display concrete artifacts and reach out and touch each student, I found students with emotional disturbances, learning disabilities, what we call ADHD, and one autistic child.

Without having any idea beforehand of any of these labels and classifications—I only knew that this was a special education classroom—I laid out a whole bunch of seashells I'd gathered from the beaches of Long Island near where Nancy and I have a house.

Well, you know what happened. The students grabbed the shells and my only word of caution was "These are a little fragile, so please let's be careful handling them." Very quickly, each student had one or more, was turning them over, and talking rapidly (some of them) about what they observed: "they're smooth on the inside . . . they come from the bottom of the ocean . . . something lived inside . . . ridges on the outside . . . different colors inside and out . . . different colors on the outside . . ." I asked on several occasions, "How do you know—they came from the bottom of the ocean . . . that creatures lived inside?"

The questions came soon after the observations:

- Why are the colors on the inside different from the outside?
- What makes the ridges?
- Who created these?

Then one student expressed his hypothesis: "I think that somebody created these and then they lived inside them."

I responded, "That's very interesting. I never thought of that. What makes you think so? " I cannot recall exactly what the boy sitting opposite me said, but he was so enthusiastic about his ideas that we went on to ask (think KWHLAQ as well as OTQ), "How can we find out?" And the students listed several resources including www.google and www.ask.com.

Now, I knew these were called scallop shells and that scallops, which live in both the ocean and bay, are sea creatures that you can dine on at home or in a restaurant. In the Milstein Hall of Ocean Life at the American Museum of Natural History in New York City, there is an entire wall full of models of invertebrates, creatures without backbones. On another wall, there are vertebrates.

As part of the former display, there is a terrific film of these scallops zooming all around the sandy ocean bottom propelled by the water they take in and then discharge, illustrating Newton's Third Law of Motion—for every action there is an equal and opposite reaction.

I don't think my young questioner had any idea of self-propulsion, but I wondered if he was onto something. Do scallops create their shells and then live in them? Exactly how does this process proceed? I've worked with these shells for many years and never thought to ask that question. The lesson learned here? Sometimes our students challenge us to think about what we take for granted or entirely ignore. Just like Keevan's question: "Why are school buses always yellow?"

A UNIT OF INSTRUCTION—WITH SPECIAL EDUCATION STUDENTS INTEGRATED

In Chapter 4, I mentioned Kelly Guzman and her colleagues at the Joseph D. Sharp Elementary School in Cherry Hill, New Jersey. Their students were very intrigued by the nature of communities and the goods and services communities needed. This was the problematic scenario that engaged her second graders:

> Hurricane Katrina destroyed the city of New Orleans. Your town was chosen as a model community to help rebuild. Think about how your town and other towns meet the needs of its citizens. Come up with a plan to rebuild New Orleans as a working community. Your plan will be presented to the town council for approval.

Kelly and her colleagues introduced the unit with pictures of communities and of the devastating effects on New Orleans of Hurricane Katrina. Her students generated many questions including:

- How do you build a community? How do they start?
- How do we know what a community is?
- Will anyone build a community in Antarctica?
- Are special needs students in all schools?
- How did fire engines (and communities) change over time?
- Do all people have the same needs?
- How can we change to a better community?
- What did the people in New Orleans do when hurricane Katrina hit?
- How many communities helped clean up New Orleans?

Kelly and her colleagues used a wide variety of resources for this unit. These included books on historic communities (i.e., Colonial Boston) and local communities (i.e., Cherry Hill); fiction such as *Because of Winn Dixie* (Di Camillo), *Family Farm* (Locker), and *Time for Kids*; atlases and globes. They also employed a variety of learning strategies (for example, note taking in journals, parent surveys, visual formative assessments—drawing pictures of various goods and services and stating why they are necessary, and creating Venn diagrams for comparing different communities). Using these different approaches, students answered many of their questions.

Their culminating projects (the result of working on the problematic scenario) involved drawing large posters and creating brochures all as a means of demonstrating their understanding of the kinds of community services needed by New Orleans.

Kelly explained to me (via telephone and e-mail) that for her special needs students, she and her two colleagues employed a variety of approaches:

- paired reading using a variety comprehension strategies;
- drawings used to express understandings of communities, goods, and services;
- written self-assessments of their performance (reflections on being good thinkers and being reflective—"What I've learned about my strengths and weaknesses");
- Venn diagrams for comparisons and contrasts;
- support and information from parents;
- paired culminating projects.

As you can see, Kelly, Denise, and Christine used a variety of interpersonal, visual, and written strategies to help their students with special needs. One special needs student's understanding of the goods, services, and needs of a community was limited to drawing a school and a house.

Kelly told me that one element in the framework we've just discussed is the importance identifying the very important concepts or ideas within a topic. This is not, I think, tantamount to doing a task analysis—breaking down complex topics into their smaller parts. What Kelly has emphasized is taking the issue to its core—what are the essential elements of a community? As I used to ask teachers, "If you had one week to teach your course, what would be the most important aspects of the subject you want to teach?"

In a final summation, all Kelly's students were genuinely surprised and, perhaps, a little saddened to learn that we hadn't made more progress in rebuilding New Orleans. This, I submit, is a testament to the extent to which her second graders took this unit on the nature of communities seriously and personally. They obviously became meaningfully involved in attempting to understand and solve an authentic problem.

UNIT OF INSTRUCTION—FOR SPECIAL NEEDS STUDENTS

Kerry Faber taught a social studies unit to her fourth-grade class of special needs students in Edmonton. Her group is comprised of students with communication delays. These students may be functioning one or two years below grade level in literacy and/or mathematics. During this unit, she used a wide array of learning experiences all of which culminated in their completing the initial challenge presented in her problematic scenario.

Here is Kerry's social studies unit in outline form:

Central idea:
Cultures in history

Supporting ideas/processes:
Aboriginal cultures living in Alberta, Canada
Comparative cultures
Inquiry in history

Problematic scenario:
"If you were transported into the past and were given a choice, would you choose to be an aboriginal living in a village or a European living in a fort? Give several valid reasons why."

Objectives:
By the end of the unit, students should be able to

1. Identify important characteristics of aboriginal cultures in Alberta.

2. Identify important characteristics of European settlements.

3. Compare, contrast, and draw conclusions about aboriginal and European cultures in Alberta in the nineteenth century.

4. Construct models of different settlements used by aboriginals and Europeans and explain major components.

5. Choose which culture they would rather live in and give good reasons.

6. Reflect on asking questions and searching for answers.

Strategies:
I usually think of a long-range plan as divided into Initial Core and Culminating Experiences.

Initiating experiences:

1. KWL chart on what students thought they knew about aboriginals.

2. Eliciting students' questions from Kerry's extensive and varied collection of pictures of aboriginal settlements.

Core learning experiences:

1. We took virtual tours of some of the heritage sites shown in the textbook. The neat thing was that some students had been to these places so we could draw on their background knowledge.

2. We took a field trip to Fort Edmonton and had a guest in to give us info about aboriginal life. I had computer CDs and used various Web sites with useful content.

3. To heighten their interest in the study of, first the aboriginals (before European influence) and then the European traders who built the fort, I told them that we would build large models of what we had learned. This really improved their attention to detail! Every subject area was included.

4. We learned the round dance in Phys-ed. We used shape and space outcomes from math to construct teepees and fort buildings.

5. We used coordinate mapping because the models were built on a large carpet marked out as a hundreds board.

6. Many art projects were involved—from designing the teepee covers to representing the three levels of Earth (space/sky, animal life, and land formations) to creating winter counts on canvas "animal skins" to represent plausible important events in their lives as aboriginal children.

7. They read many different texts and I used read-aloud novels that they responded to in journal entries.

8. I posed different levels of questions for them to respond to and many of them posed "I wonder" and "Why" questions that we made predictions for and researched.

9. They wrote journal entries that included "a day in my life as an aboriginal . . ." to share their levels of understanding. (This was done once the village model was completed, so they had lots to look at to help stimulate ideas.)" (K. Faber, personal communication, April, 2007)

Many of the students' questions arose as they read about aboriginal and European settlements in Alberta:

- Why are the teepees black at the top? (Textbook pictures showed most of the tents as white with noticeably black areas at the very top.)

- Why would the Europeans want to take away the land the aboriginals had chosen in the treaty? Didn't they already have enough? Why couldn't they share better?

- If the Manitou Stone [a meteorite] was so important to the aboriginals, why did the Europeans take it away from them?

Culminating project:

1. Building models of both aboriginal settlements and European forts

2. Writing letters expressing their choices with good reasons

In her reflections on this unit, Kerry shared these thoughts with me: I had very little difficulty getting them to write because they had so much background knowledge due to the active research. They required little encouragement to research aspects of aboriginal or fort life because they knew that, the more they learned, the more they could choose to include in the large floor model!

It was intriguing to hear how they would problem solve to figure out how to construct a travois or a backrest or a drying rack for meat. One child would figure out how to create something and then others would go over to check it out and try that design. It was interesting to see how some children figured they were really good at building one particular thing and made multiple copies to then "trade" with others for what they were making. Children brought in small models to add to the display with the understanding that these had to fit to scale and be valid objects found during that time.

As much as possible, I tried to be a facilitator and encourage them to seek help from each other instead of getting me to help. When they asked me a question, I posed another one to get them started in the right direction to find the answer on their own or with a peer.

The final product turned out to be much bigger and more detailed than I had imagined. It also took a lot longer—but, because I had continually included other subject objectives in lessons, I covered a great deal of the curriculum! Parents stopped by to check out the progress because their children talked about what they were doing. Teachers and students from other class-rooms popped in occasionally to check out the progress. We have an aboriginal liaison fellow in our school and when he came to see the village, he was very impressed and verified many of the facts that the children shared.

Kerry also noted that other teachers visited her classroom to observe the progress her students were making in building the two models.

Here are copies of some of their final letters:

Dear Ms. Dolby,

I have been studying about life in Alberta's past. If I were given a choice between living as an Aboriginal in a village or a European in the fort, I would choose to be an Aboriginal man. First, I would be free to go off and hunt whenever I want. I would hunt with a bow and arrow. Second, I don't have to be stuck in a building. I can go outside. Finally, I would travel all the time on our migration route. I like going to Writing on Stone.

These are the reasons why I would want to be a Aboriginal if I lived in the past.

Yours Truly,

M . . .

Kerry explains, "This boy has significant academic challenges yet, he is often one of my most insightful students! This is due largely to the fact that he has parents who spend a great deal of time exposing him to many experiences. He has been to many of the heritage sites we have studied. Some of his family are Metis, so he has been exposed to his aboriginal ancestry. He learns best when he is given very multi-experiential opportunities."

Dear Ms. Dolby,

I have been studying about life in Alberta's past. If I were given a choice between living as an Aboriginal in a village or a European. I would choose to be an Aboriginal girl. First, you get a knife when you are 3 or 4 so you can help your brothers.

Second, Aboriginal people who spoke different languages often met up with each other. This was especially so on the plains where horses made travel easier. Finally, in times of need people often served because communities helped each other and shared what they had .

These are the reasons why I would what to be an Aboriginal girl if I lived in the past.

Your friend,

M . . .

"This girl is very quiet in class but can be quite reflective when the topic is meaningful to her."

And, finally, this letter from one of her stronger academic yet not as articulate students:

Dear Ms. Dolby,

I have been studying about life in Alberta's past. If I were given a choice between living as an Aboriginal in a village or a European in the fort, I would choose to be an Aboriginal boy. First, I would like to travel on the migration Route. I would like to travel to Writing On Stone. Second, I would get freedom and people in the fort didn't get freedom. I would get to play on the land. Third, I would get my knife when I am three or four. People in the fort got their knifes when they were five. Finally, I can go to the Buffalo Jump to hunt Buffalo. We would get a lot of Buffalo. These are the reasons why I would want Aboriginal boy if I live in the past.

Sincerely,

T . . .

(Edmonton Public Schools, 2007)[1]

As you can see, these letters provide evidence of students' learning about the different cultures of Native Americans and Europeans living in Alberta. I asked Kerry what criteria she used to assess students' learning from these various experiences and she mentioned the following:

1. Ability to work collaboratively

2. Class participation

3. Kinds of questions asked (and ability to suggest/get answers)

4. Ability to support conclusions with "valid" information

5. Ability to make connections

In addition, Kerry noted that she expects her special needs students "to demonstrate their learning in three modalities—orally, in written form and through some visual form (i.e., model, display, etc.)" Notice how she's using the basic principles of effective assessment—challenging students to demonstrate understanding in more than one form of personal expression. Some students may excel at writing, but others may feel more comfortable building something or using an art form.

You will note that the latter three items just mentioned involve critical thinking: drawing reasonable conclusions. Asking good questions is

---

[1] © Reproduced with permission from Edmonton Public Schools.

certainly part of leading us toward such judgments and I would hope it is part of how we assess our students in all classes.

It might be of particular interest that here we have an attempt to challenge students to state ideas, give reasons for these ideas, and seek out connections to other content. As we noted in Chapter 2, when students seek relationships with other ideas, they demonstrate to us the degree to which they understand content. Making connections is how we make ideas meaningful, and the more extensive these relationships are the more meaningful the learning (Johnson, 1975).

CONCLUSION

As we can see from Kerry and Kelly's units involving special education students, they are fully capable of becoming very excited about learning different cultures as well as any other subject that is part of the regular curriculum.

I hope that the models presented in this chapter highlight the following elements, which are part of the special education classroom:

- Focus on **problematic situations**
- Sufficient **time** to explore novelties and strange, perplexing situations
- Access to multiple and **alternative** resources, print, media, and so forth
- Students having input and **shared control** over decision making
- Supportive **structures** that help students work through the inquiry and research processes
- Focusing on **key elements/concepts** within the curriculum
- Having alternative ways of expressing or performing their understandings

We know that Michelle's, Kerry's, and Liz's students have very significant challenges and I for one have always had the deepest admiration and respect for educators like them who devote so much time and energy to helping specially challenged students to perform well.

As a teacher/educator for many years, I often found myself sharing what teachers of these students do with the wider audience of school faculty; conducting task analyses with content subjects; using multiple modalities for learning and reporting; and sharing control of decision making with their students.

In summary, this comment by one teacher seems appropriate:

> My students can do just about anything the other students can do. It just might take a little longer.

We all have much to learn from all our students, perhaps especially from those with special needs.

PRACTICAL OPPORTUNITIES

1. Which of the many and varied kinds of learning modes/styles do your students benefit most of all?

2. Which students need more time and a different way to access information and share it?

3. What can we learn from how these special education teachers work with their students that we can use to engage all of our students—e.g., use of time, access to different resources, control of decision making, reliance on higher structures, more clearly delineated procedures, and ways of sharing what they've learned?

4. What have we learned from our students with special needs from their questions, their ways of learning, and their ideas and conclusions?

OTHER AUTHENTIC ASSESSMENTS

Michelle Thoemke's second-grade special needs class wrote a newspaper at the conclusion of their unit on understanding animals. They dictated the stories, she typed them, and they found pictures to illustrate the stories.

Here's the rubric she used for this culminating experience:

Summative Assessment Rubric

1.	Name of living thing	WOW!	OK	SO-SO	OOPS
2.	Classification (reptile, mammal, bird, amphibian, fish, plant)				
3.	Life cycle Used pictures or words				
4.	Wrote about animal				
5.	Project is neat				

Name: _____   Date: _____

Professional Development Beyond Our Classrooms

FINDING THE RIGHT NEED

Years ago while teaching English at Thomas Jefferson High School in Brooklyn, New York (near Isidore I. Rabi's home of many years earlier), I wanted to become better at what I did in the classroom and wanted to share what I was doing with colleagues.

One of the first outreaches for professional growth was driving with Nancy from New York City to a workshop in the Washington, D.C. area where for two days I learned how to create something called a Learning Activity Package, which involved setting clear objectives for students' learning and developing a variety of strategies for students to achieve success. We were striving to help all students become successful by clearly defining our intended outcomes for students' learning and by using a wide variety of approaches to reach these instructional goals. The basic principle, I now realize, was what we've just witnessed in working with special education students—that we all learn in different ways and at different paces.

This experience transformed my way of teaching. As I've mentioned earlier, I used to teach *Macbeth* by laying out lesson plan after lesson plan and then at the end of the play, asking, "What and how will I assess students' learning?"

By specifying the objectives beforehand, we all had a set of observable goals toward which to work. For example, I knew that students would need to identify major elements of the plot and analyze the major characters' actions/words and explain Shakespeare's use of symbol and metaphor ("Life's but a walking shadow . . .").

After rearranging my instructional plans with students—having very specific intended outcomes—I decided that I wanted to share this new technology with friends in the English Department. I approached my department chair, Milton Katz, and he gave me time at a monthly after-school department meeting. I shared the essence of Learning Activity Packages and the only response I recall many years later is, "Seems like a lot more work."

Well, yes, in the short run.

What I learned was that no new approach would resonate with people unless it met a specific instructional need. My colleagues were happy teaching in their accustomed ways and no one ever visited my classroom.

On another occasion, I was working in the alternative school at Jefferson and experimenting with portable videotape cameras, making films with students on any subject they wanted. Some were crime dramas; one was a documentary of our explorations of the Catskill Mountains in New York and its beaches on Long Island. Back then, you had a hand-held camera and a briefcase-sized Portapak with reel-to-reel tape and a large battery inside, which you had to carry up and down the mountains on your shoulder.

Once again, I shared this technology with colleagues and someone said, "So, you've got your captive audience, John." Again, no questions until a year later one teacher saw a need for kids to express themselves in other ways and she asked to walk around with me as we made a film and then she tried it with her students as well.

REFLECTIVE PAUSE

What do these episodes tell you about teacher growth using alternative approaches? One thing I learned from these experiences is that people will stretch themselves into new areas to solve observed problems in their classrooms. I found that my students at Thomas Jefferson were often bored and not learning as I wanted. Perhaps there were ways to meet their individual needs by learning new teaching approaches. After service in the U.S. Navy, I took requisite graduate courses to become licensed in New York City, and there had been only one Methods of Teaching course during the summer at Hunter College. I needed to expand my repertoire dramatically.

The basic principle here is that effective school change is that which meets real instructional needs and helps solve identified problems related to students' learning. Too much school change is characterized by our implementing various solutions to problems we haven't identified. Why, for example, was cooperative learning so vital once upon a time? What was the problem it was solving? Too many of us are chasing solutions to problems no one has defined clearly.

How is this lesson on the importance of identifying instructional needs important for teaching inquiry?

We will be enthusiastic about challenging students to ask good questions, conduct research, think critically, and draw reasonable conclusions when we think and feel that students' participating in this process helps them become more actively engaged in their learning (not passive), to be in more control of their own progress (not allowing adults to make all of the decisions), and to achieve what they want in life (including becoming a concert pianist, an author, an NBA player, or a college professor).

In other words, does inquiry-based instruction meet real classroom needs about learning and succeeding in life? I hope we have identified some ways in which inquiry helps students achieve (see Chapter 2).

So, assuming you have identified some instructional needs within your classroom, what are some ways you can learn about effective solutions?

NETWORKING WITH COLLEAGUES

Virtually every success book—how to get what you want out of life—contains chapters on envisioning a new life, setting goals, believing in your eventual success, and living to see the rewards. Jack Canfield, one author of the original Chicken Soup books, expressed it this way during a recent teleseminar, "Conceive, Believe and Achieve" (accessed 18 April, 2007): This means set a vision for yourself (articulate with clearly defined goals), believe you can attain it and by working hard toward that vision reap the rewards of achievement. No one is suggesting this process is a passive experience.

Here are some ways of working toward our visions for success.

Part of this process is networking with people of similar attitudes about teaching and learning. This means finding those educators who are doing things in their classrooms that we'd like to learn more about and, perhaps, experimenting with those ideas within our own classrooms.

Classroom Visits

In Edmonton, Kerry Faber takes advantage of opportunities to visit other classrooms and learn from colleagues. Sometimes districts schedule professional development days during which teachers with ideas and approaches demonstrate their successes with colleagues. This is one of the very best ways to enhance our own learning and to meet instructional needs. But we know from research on successful schools that teachers' visiting each others' classrooms is one of the major characteristics leading to such productivity. Just being in a different setting watching teachers and students work toward similar goals can be eye opening for all of us.

When I was a teacher in New York City, I did not spend much time in other people's classrooms, nor can I remember participating in the kinds of faculty meetings where the focus was on instructional approaches. But at Montclair State University, I had the good fortune to learn from many of my colleagues how they fostered thinking in the classroom by visiting these classes, discussing what we had videotaped, and then composing the findings into a modest little book called *Opening the American Mind* (1988).

We don't need to go through this kind of extensive process to learn from our colleagues. I will long remember how one professor brought students back from daydreaming, how another taught students to listen carefully lest he err, how another structured his teaching about the eye in a most logical fashion, and, finally, how another modeled his own inquisitiveness about a Robert Frost poem. My teaching thereafter was enriched many fold.

Electronic Networking

Other ways to network include using e-mails to communicate with a group of like-minded persons. For example, in one New Jersey middle school, Jane Kinkle and colleagues (including one principal) determined that they wanted to learn how to apply the principles of Gardner's Multiple Intelligences to their students, specifically those with ADD (Barell, 2003, p. 218). Jane and her colleagues spent several weeks asking and answering questions in a continuous "threaded discussion" via an e-mail network set up for this purpose by the district. Here's one telling response:

> I really feel that the MI approach was made for the ADD, social and/or disruptive child . . . Recently, I did a lesson where the kinesthetic intelligence played a big role in learning to remember facts . . . one usually disruptive child really got into the actions associated with the list and when it came time to recall them he was right on the mark . . . (p. 219)

This experience was, I think, occasioned by many of the faculty of this school in Caldwell having a prior experience with Multiple Intelligences, perhaps through a workshop given by another teacher or an outside consultant.

Helen Teague, an expert on how to network electronically and founder of one of the best teacher resources on the Web (www.oops.biz-land.com), suggests a number of other ways to network electronically:

1. Sign up for resources and e-newsletters at education power-houses such as Edutopia, Blue Web'n, ASCD, Teaching Tolerance Web site, and Refdesk.com.

2. Correspond with another teacher of the same grade in another state. EPals and Keypals are a great site for initiating correspondence or networking when at a conference.

3. Submit a lesson idea or lesson plan to educational sites to become a published educator. Then build a shared community among these educators.

Corresponding with other teachers via e-mail can be a most rewarding experience. So many of the stories in this book have come from e-mails after initial visits in schools.

Sharing Best Practices at Faculty Meetings

One day I was speaking with a curriculum leader in a school and a teacher walked in the room to share what he'd just gotten from one of his second graders, a long written piece about the mystery of the disappearing bees. It seems as if in recent months our bee population around the world has been steadily dwindling.

> Where have all the bees gone? Beekeepers, researchers, and farmers are buzzing. They want to know why millions of honeybees are disappearing. The bees are leaving no clues and no dead bodies behind. "The bees have vanished," says Jerry Bromenshenk, a bee expert. (*Time for Kids*, March, 16, 2007, p. 2)

The teacher, I'll call him Bill, was excited because the day before he'd read the story and challenged his students to go home and find out why the bees are missing. One student had gotten information from the Internet and written it down. When I visited the class, another student told us her mom thought it had to do with global warming. Another student had another idea and I asked where he got it from. "I Googled it," he said. I asked if the school regularly had best-practice sharing sessions for Bill to discuss what he had done and was told that they occasionally did.

This, it seems to me, is one key to our professional growth, networking with members of our own faculty, learning from each other, not only over the lunch table, but at regular meetings where we showcase what one or more teachers are doing, perhaps visiting their classrooms to see what students have been producing.

In *School Leadership that Works* (2005) Marzano, Waters, and McNulty identify several responsibilities of good, effective leadership teams. The first responsibility is affirmation—"the extent to which the leader recognizes and celebrates school accomplishments—and acknowledges failures" (p. 41). One way to do this is to "take time in staff meetings to share and celebrate individual and school-wide learning (successes and failures)" (p. 117).

Clearly communicating our successes in meeting our instructional goals is, obviously, one key element in developing an effective school (http://www.nwrel.org/scpd/esp/esp95.html#2.1.1 accessed April, 2007).

(By the way, my wife recently heard that cell phone activity has contributed to the bee disappearance. Now how would be test this out?)

Professional Walkthroughs

Principals sometimes engage in professional development experiences called "walkthroughs," wherein they visit another school and are shown around by the principal to observe, learn what's going on, and provide guidance. It seems like an excellent process that we teachers ought to be engaged in as well, first within our own buildings and then within others. We can get substitutes for our classes or we can arrange for coverage for perhaps a period of one or more hours of such networking visitations. There's nothing like visiting another classroom and school to provide a brief respite from our own routines and to open our eyes to other ways of doing things.

Sometimes when I model inquiry in a K–6 classroom I'm surprised at some of the debriefing comments: "I never would have thought of getting them out of their chairs . . . to make a game of it . . . to have them solve the problem without a precise model in mind . . . to use the cover of the book to model my own inquisitiveness . . . not to use the textbook as my main resource."

All it takes is to witness somebody else working with our curriculum in a different fashion to raise questions such as, "What if I did it that way?" or "What if I try this approach with my own special modifications?"

One of the things we know about sharing visits, about what some people call "peer coaching," is that such practices can have a positive impact on our teaching practices. Teachers engaged in such a process "practiced new skills and strategies more frequently and applied them more appropriately than did their counterparts who worked alone to expand their repertoires" (Showers & Joyce, 1996, p. 14).

Melissa Anderson-Rossini of Whittier International Elementary School in Minneapolis recently commenced such a peer observation process with teachers. Acting as the IB coordinator she encouraged pairs of teachers to share visits. What helped teachers overcome their initial reluctance was Melissa's challenge to observe what the students were doing. That was each teacher's focus in her colleague's classroom and this facilitated the peer sharing process. (Anderson-Rossini, 2007, personal communication).

Attending and Presenting at Conferences

Of course, we all network when we meet friends and colleagues in large groups, at district meetings of all faculty, or at local and regional conferences. One of the delights of attending conferences is to meet presenters who have wonderful ideas to share. Another idea, which is even more exciting, is to become a presenter yourself and to network with people who attend your session.

Sometimes we don't think that what we are doing is very different from what others are doing and, therefore, it is not worth sharing. We get butterflies whenever we think about sharing ideas with colleagues. This is far more nerve wracking than working all day with a group of fourth graders!

However, if you have been working successfully with an approach or with materials that you think get students actively engaged, inquiring, and working toward solid culminating projects and/or assessments, you should think about how to share your ideas with others.

LEADERSHIP TEAMS

Ronda Borchert, the principal of George P. Nicholson School in Edmonton, decided one day to engage her faculty in professional development by reading what she hoped would be an enlightening book. She asked for volunteers to become leaders to take on this project. They read the book during the course of several months, discussed it chapter by chapter, and when I walked into this school a couple of years ago, there were flipchart papers taped to various walls with recorded comments and questions about the text. In this case, they happened to have read *Developing More Curious Minds* (Barell, 2003) and the one chapter I remember seeing was on assessment.

Here was another marvelous, safe, and secure way to network within your own building and to share ideas in a comfortable setting supported by the principal. Not all principals lead in this way nor are all interested in this kind of focus on inquiry. Fortunately for the teachers at George P. Nicholson school, they have a principal who is always modeling her own inquisitiveness with "I wonder statements" and I wish I had been a fly on the wall during some of those discussions.

INQUIRY JOURNALS

Jodi Baker is the International Baccalaureate coordinator at Evergreen Park World Studies Elementary School in Brooklyn Center, Minnesota. Visiting her school was a marvelous experience not only of modeling in a wide variety of classrooms, but also of feeling the direct support of the faculty. Jodi introduced me at an early morning one-hour professional development workshop before classes and when I opened my mouth everybody knew that I had lost my voice, had a cold coming on, or was otherwise in mild distress. Within five minutes, one teacher brought me a week's supply of cough drops and that made all the difference.

Jodi has worked with her faculty over the past two years on an Inquiry Journal project. At least once a month, she meets with her teachers and they share what they've been wondering about and what they've been learning about the inquiry process. Obviously, her principal Jill Griffith-McRaith has supported Jodi's efforts with time, space, and other resources.

Erin is a fourth-grade teacher at Evergreen Park Elementary School in Brooklyn Center, Minnesota. Here is her Wonder Journal entry for October, 26, 2006:

> Appreciating the perspectives of people in faraway lands seems relatively easy for me. These individuals and groups have experiences of a completely other life than that which I've lived. I expect their ideas and perceptions to look different from mine. How couldn't they?
>
> But showing (and honestly feeling) open-mindedness toward the differing perspectives and opinions of those close to me is likely one of my greatest struggles. I could dialogue all day long with an Al Queda member about our differing political and religious perspectives, but I've rarely been able to do the same thing with my own father.
>
> Why is it so hard to share ideas with my dad? What stops us from communicating effectively? Are there underlying concepts I hold that hinder me from hearing him? How does that "communication failure" with him impact my effectiveness at listening to and respecting my students, colleagues, parents, etc.?

Erin continues by explaining how she structures her Wonder Journal:

The way I try to structure my wonder journal entries is three-fold. I write on a topic I'm interested in/have on my mind/recently had brought to my attention. Then I intentionally read through those ramblings a few times and respond with questions that are generally reflective about whatever I've written. Sometimes my questions are simple perspective-type ones like "Where could I find a differing view on the 3M chemical pollution in East Metro groundwater?" (a significant story in the Twin Cities area). Often times, however, my questions tend to be more reflective of my own thinking: "What drew me to this story/idea?" "How does this poem express my struggles with language, parent-teacher partnerships, friendships, etc.? (e-mail, April, 2007)

> "Sometimes my questions are simple perspective-type ones like 'Where could I find a differing view on the 3M chemical pollution in East Metro groundwater' (a significant story in the Twin Cities area)."
>
> *Erin Kelly, fourth-grade teacher, Brooklyn Center, MN*

It will be obvious to all readers that having Erin for a teacher is a marvelous experience! I can imagine so many occasions where she shares these speculations and wonderings with her students.

ELECTRONIC NETWORKING

Peggy Bumanis was a second-grade teacher in Edmonton who took a special online course through the American Museum of Natural History. This course, called a Seminar on Science (http://learn.amnh.org), focused on geology and was called "Earth: Inside and Out." Here are Peggy's reflections:

Not having a strong science background (which became very evident during this course!) I found it to be a real challenge—as well, the students in the course came from a wide background (always a good thing) but also from varying degrees of background knowledge—there were some PhD students in my group for example. Deciding not to "bail," I did finish it and certainly expanded my science knowledge—the online dialogue was great and because we knew a bit about each other, it became easier to connect with others teaching same grades and with relatively speaking, same background knowledge—therefore became a valuable experience. It was really fascinating to have people from all over the place in my online group sharing parts of their experiences and curriculum. (e-mail, 20 April, 2007)

Peggy experienced one of the major benefits of taking such courses: networking people in similar roles. She found other elementary teachers in this Seminar on Science course and communicated with them, most likely, outside the parameters of the major "threaded discussions" that provide the main forum for sharing ideas. It is a tribute to Peggy's perseverance that she kept at it, and did not "bail," as she said.

WHAT DO WE DO WITH A RELUCTANT PRINCIPAL?

Jill Levine, principal of the Normal Park Museum Magnet School in Chattanooga, is a dynamic leader of an inquiry-based school. Her students engage in nine-week units much like Robin Cayce's World War II unit described in Chapter 1.

I have first-hand knowledge of how she guides her teachers toward inquiry, ensuring that they have sufficient resources, can access knowledge beyond their classrooms, and have time for collaboration. One of the neatest ideas she generated last year was something called a Travel Journal. Here was a notebook in which students could write down their assignments, their current questions about a topic, as well as their findings. She asked a small group of teachers if they thought this was a good idea.

The response was "yes." After a short period of field-testing, these teachers shared what they'd been doing with all of their colleagues and the school decided to adopt Travel Journals in all of its classrooms. What a marvelous opportunity for reflection after a unit, after a year, and after five or six years, assuming we keep all of these journals.

Why am I talking about Jill here? Because she suggested that a good topic to write about would be "What do we do with a principal who hasn't bought into the idea of inquiry?" Or one whose leadership is what you might call laissez-faire?

Once Again, the Need Factor

Recall our opening conversation about the importance of meeting real instruction needs as the sine qua non of successful school change. If we are solving observable learning problems, then our ideas have a better chance of being accepted. So, here are some steps we can take if we are working with a reluctant leader:

A. Identify real learning needs we have in our classrooms (e.g., learning different subjects, achievement on tests, mastering specific content concepts and skills managing student behavior, and the like).

B. Determine which strategies you are using that are helping to transform your classrooms from environments where students are sitting passively accepting knowledge from you to ones wherein they are actively engaged in questioning, researching, and sharing new knowledge.

C. Share some of these with your principal.

   1. Invite him or her in to witness what you are doing and discuss with students why they are engaged.

   2. Meet to discuss what you are doing, sharing some students' products and data reflecting achievement.

D. Ask to share some of these approaches with other teachers:

   1. Within grade level meetings: Follow Kelly's lead and voluntarily congregate to discuss what you are doing and discuss how it is solving various kinds of problems related to learning. (In effect, forming your own teaching teams)

   2. Volunteer to share with the entire faculty at a regular faculty meeting. Follow Kerry's example wherein at every faculty meeting teachers are invited to share a best practice with colleagues who sign up to visit and carry on the conversation afterwards.

E. You might not call such a meeting a Best Practice Session, I know. Most of us would not want to parade ourselves and our ideas as Best Practice, because we know how that would appear to our colleagues. We might just say, "Here's what my students have been doing. This is the kind of work I used to get. Now, as students become more actively engaged with inquiry, problem solving, critical thinking, and reflection, this is the kind of work they are presenting." Let everybody ask questions.

F. To the degree that this initial process is successful, we might engage in it on successive occasions. We might also ask the principal to do the following:

   1. Include notes on effective approaches in the school newsletter and correspondence with parents.

2. Encourage other teachers to send work home that reflects the effective approaches you are using.

3. Invite interested parents in to meet with teachers, visit class-rooms, and consider broadening use of such approaches in other classrooms.

The issue of sharing ideas with colleagues can raise questions about image and self-importance, but we can deal with this by focusing on real classroom needs. It's not a matter of whose ideas are better. It's a question of "How do our approaches deal with real instructional issues, problems, and difficulties?" The important thing is to always focus on the data, just as with observe, think, and question. What do we see? What is observable in our classrooms?

All real change deals with classroom issues that we approach with a problem-identification and problem-solving frame of mind (see Fullan, 1991, 1993). Too much change results from everybody's pet ideas, cur-rent trends, and slick marketing strategies from Madison Avenue. Successful changes meet problematic situations head on and deal with approaches that actually make a difference. Thus, having students' data in the form of formative and summative assessments is very, very important.

As a resident of New York City, I've noticed several administrative changes recently, from local districts to regions and back to districts. I'm always wondering, "What differences do any of these changes make in the interactions amongst teachers and students?"

IDENTIFYING THE NEED

Another alternative was one pursued in an elementary school where I worked over a period of two or more years (River Edge, New Jersey). A group of teachers gathered to help identify instructional needs and share them with the board of education. They developed a series of informal needs assessment written activities related to major intellectual processes such as problem solving, which they believed was important for their stu-dents to develop over time.

They administered a brief, written assessment (Barell, 1995) devel-oped by my colleague Irving Sigel at Educational Testing Service, Princeton, New Jersey. The assessment read something like this: "Bobby received a new train for his birthday. It worked well for a while, but then stopped working. Write a brief paragraph about how you would respond to this situation." We administered this in grades three through six.

What we found was that some students merely wrote down, "I'd give it to my dad to fix."

But others, in the minority, went through a complex process of identifying what could be wrong—the tracks, the electricity, the engine, and so forth—to eliminate the possible causes. From this, with the principal's and the board's approval, we created a teacher-designed program fostering those intellectual skills related to problem solving, critical thinking, and taking responsibility for thinking on your own.

Here is another example of the rational approach to school change—conduct a needs assessment, analyze findings, draw conclusions, and take action.

WITHOUT MONEY, TIME, OR PUBLIC SUPPORT

But what if we have more reluctance than I've previously assumed? What if we are working with leaders who have other priorities or who are, at best, laissez-faire in their management approaches?

Networking

If this is the case, we should follow Kelly's lead and voluntarily meet with colleagues to share needs and valued approaches.

Electronic Outreach

There's no impediment to our following Peggy's lead and taking courses online or at graduate schools to advance our basic content knowledge. I've taught the latter kinds of courses for years, mostly for teachers who were seeking additional certifications to become supervisors and/or principals.

However, we do not need to take a full six-week course such as a seminar. We can network with those who have hosted Web sites full of helpful information about teaching and learning and about inquiry-based instruction. Here are some sites:

Teacher Resources

A general site for excellent teacher approaches is Helen Teague's www.oops.bizland.com.

Webquests uses problematic scenarios to launch Internet-based inquiries: http://www.spa3.k12.sc.us/WebQuests.html. Some quests reflect the essence of the problematic scenarios previously discussed.

You can find out more by visiting Kathy Schrock's Guide for webquests and the The 1960's Museum: http://school.discovery.com/schrockguide/museum/webquest.html. If you consider using such a museum context, as I've used in many classes, you should not only ask students to find suitable exhibits but also to justify/explain why they've made their selections, so we know they understand their importance.

Home of Problem-Based Learning Initiative describes the work of Dr. Howard Barrow, an originator of concept for medical education: http://www.pbli.org/

You can find more information at the Illinois Math and Science Academy: http://www.imsa.edu/

Various Content Sites

The American Museum of Natural History is a logical place to begin searches involving science and natural history: www.amnh.org. Ology, a Web site from AMNH for young explorers: www.ology.amnh.org. Seminars on Science: http://learn.amnh.org/ And for all educational resources available at AMNH: www.amnh.org/resources.

Polar exploration, Antarctica: http://www.exploratorium.edu/poles/index.html. See Adelies, icebreakers in McMurdo, Mt. Erebus (only active volcano in Antarctica), and South Pole Station.

Astronomy for kids: http://www.kidsastronomy.com/ Lots of interesting descriptions of stars, galaxies, black holes, and much more. See also Ology.

NASA's Imagine the Universe: http://imagine.gsfc.nasa.gov/ Up-to-date information and photos from Hubble and other telescopes with breaking news such as the following about planets beyond our solar system:

NASA's Spitzer Space Telescope has captured for the first time enough light from planets outside our solar system to identify molecules in their atmospheres. The landmark achievement is a significant step toward being able to detect possible life on rocky exoplanets and comes years before astronomers had anticipated (News item, accessed April, 2007).

SECURITY IN NUMBERS

One of the oldest change strategies is based on the principle that there's strength and security in numbers. This means that if a sufficient core of teachers has been working with successful strategies for a while these teachers might want to consider making their case as a group to the principal, always keeping in mind that you want to present the problem identification and resolving model:

> Here's the problem as we see it—students' achievement, behavior . . .
> Here are the questions we've been asking . . .

These are some solutions we're working on . . .

And these are some of our findings . . . (show students' work)

This is known as the "rational approach" to change because it is, again, based on what we can directly observe in the classroom—excited students who are actively asking questions, accessing information, doing well on assessments, and scoring well on those standardized examinations. It is not reflective of a pet idea, some fad, or a marketing approach by a bookseller, but is based on solid data from the classroom.

If it works, why not share it?

I know of one principal who used a strategy like this: Ronda Borchert in Edmonton. When called on to explain and justify her work on inquiry to the city board of education, she said, "I'll let the students do it." And she did. Sixth graders made their presentations directly to the board explaining how inquiry worked and why it was successful. I see this as similar to teachers making such a presentation to the principal, because in both cases we're dealing with what's occurring in the classroom.

CONCLUSION

The very first principle in Jack Canfield's book *The Success Principles* (2005) is this: Take 100% responsibility for your life (p. 3).

This means that we are in control of our lives, our decisions, and our quality of life. No blaming and pointing fingers at others, no saying "I can't do this," and no spouting lengthy excuses for being mired in a dead-end position. This means no stories of victimization wherein we are silent sufferers and victims of somebody else's skullduggery.

What Canfield, and all others who study success in life, is referring to is that we realize we can make certain decisions to improve the nature of our lives and that we need to recognize our responsibility for the situations we are in. What we control is not only our goal setting and decision making, but, equally important, our responses to events. If somebody accidentally hits our car in the parking lot, we can rant and rave and allow it to spoil our day or week, or, we can take a different approach—filing the necessary accident reports, getting the damage fixed, and moving on. What we've been discussing in this chapter are various ways that we take control of our professional lives.

> **Kelly** voluntarily bands together with colleagues to share ideas.

> **Kerry** mentors new teachers and invites others in to see what she's doing.

> **Teachers in River Edge, New Jersey**, took control of their own professional development instead of leaving it up to others.

And so might we change the course of our professional lives in so many different ways. All we need to do is decide on our own growth, set a goal, visualize it intently (daily), and work tirelessly toward it. Sounds simple, and in actuality, it really is.

Remember, Michelle, who realized that she was the limiting factor on what her special education students could do. Once she recognized this negative limitation, she changed her point of view to "There's no limit to what my students can do." That same attitude of positive self-image and control can be ours in terms of our professional growth.

PRACTICAL OPPORTUNITIES

1. What opportunities for professional growth exist now in my school or district?

2. How many have I experienced?

3. What alternatives can I generate for my own professional growth?

4. How can I work with colleagues to have a positive impact on the professional development programs in my school or district?

5. What decisions have I made recently to affect the quality of life in my school and in my personal life?

6. How am I now taking control of my own professional development? What has worked successfully in the past? What am I doing that's not working well? And what am I not doing that I could be doing to grow professionally? (Adapted from Canfield, 2005.)

Conclusion

JOURNEYS OF WONDER AND DISCOVERY

This has been an amazing journey of wonder, inquiry, and discovery. I have had the pleasure of working with so many gifted teachers, coordinators, and principals over the past couple of years. From California to New York, I've worked with students in kindergarten through Grade 6 in their regular classes as well as in art, music and physical education. It has also been my distinct pleasure to work with those children who have special needs.

In all of these classrooms, we have modeled the inquiry process and demonstrated ways of challenging students to ask good questions and determine how to find answers. In reflecting on all these wonderful experiences, I recall these memorable moments:

> All the children who, when asked if they had any questions for me, wanted to know "How old are you?" I let them figure it out, but when one young lady said, "18," I responded, "That's fine."

> The students in an art class who, after class, came over to give me a hug.

> The kindergartners who huddled together so tightly to figure out why Emperor penguins did the same in the dead of the Antarctic winter—"To stay warm," or as one child said, "Because they're friendly." Yes, indeed.

> The students with reading difficulties who were asking about whales' eating patterns. One young girl kept trying to formulate her question and, blessedly, I let her keep at it not knowing where she was headed. Finally, she said she wondered if all the fish a whale ate were in its belly "swimming around down there."

> The third grader who asked, "How did Diego Rivera's art change the world?" Because the unit was on "history makers," we took that question and challenged students to think of how art, in general, affects the world.

> The sixth grader who was studying culture and noted, as I used my appearance in his class as a way of initiating a discussion of dif-

ferent aspects of culture, that I was dressed appropriately for his class "but not for a hip-hop party." Indeed.

And the fourth grader who, after reading about the formation of volcanoes during which they compared the process to shaking a bottle of soda, said, "This is better than recess!"

HOW WE GET BETTER

Also at the end of this journey I received an e-mail from Liz Debrey, one of our staunchest correspondents over the past many months who has shared with us her students' working through the ancient civilizations and religion units.

At one point, I noticed such a clear improvement in their questions, from "Is this Rome?" (examining a photo of the Colosseum) to "How do grades affect employment opportunities?" I asked her to challenge her students to reflect on how they had grown in their abilities to ask questions. What explained their growth from mainly asking questions that had short answers—Level I of Three Story Intellect—to more thoughtful ones, many of which were at Level II?

First, Liz asked, "Have you become better inquirers this year?"

- Yes. I asked questions that I had to do research on.
- Yes! I have been asking more questions than I did at the beginning of the year.
- Yes! I think it's because I have gotten wiser, and I am thinking more about really hard questions.
- Yes because this year we had some pretty interesting units!
- Yes because in third grade I didn't know much, and I wasn't in tuned to asking questions.
- Yes because I started digging deep and asking questions that are really hard to answer.
- Yes because thinking more about the unit helps me ask better questions.

Note how one student says he's better because the units are more interesting. Maybe that's because the students were challenged to get involved, observe, think, and generate questions on their own that then became part of the unit. Students were expected "to do research on their curiosities and develop questions that would lead to purposeful investigations. (See Sherezeda's rubric created in sixth grade for researchable questions in Chapter 7.)

Also notice the student who says she is "digging deep and asking questions that are really hard to answer." This means that Liz has done a wonderful job of helping her students grow beyond "Is this Rome?" to "How do grades affect employment opportunities?" What we have here is quite impressive growth from Level I to Level II of the Three Story Intellect. Growth from being satisfied with answers we can read in a text to searching for relationships between today and many tomorrows hence, between school work and future rewards. Here we might have an early example of growing beyond concrete operations, as Piaget termed thinking in the early elementary grades, more toward abstract reasoning usually characteristic of students in the upper elementary grades and beyond.

WHAT ACCOUNTS FOR YOUR IMPROVEMENT?

Then Liz asked another question: "What helped you become better at asking more 'juicy' questions?"

Here are some of their answers:

- By asking my mom questions at home and being curious.
- Finding something I like, and that I don't know anything about makes me curious.
- I was interested in the themes, and wanted to learn about them.
- I learned more, which made me want to ask more important questions.
- Learning more about religion made me ask better questions about it.
- Being in school helped me ask better questions.
- Finding out something interesting, and finding out why something is the way it is.
- I think really hard and study a lot.
- Just asking so many questions in the past helped me with the current questions.
- I kept asking questions, and then deep ones came to my mind.
- By paying really close attention in class.
- In religion I really wanted to get more answers, so I asked more questions.
- Hearing other questions gave me more questions.

Again, we have a variety of reasons why students got better at asking good questions—from becoming engrossed in the themes, like religion, to paying attention in class.

What these fourth and fifth graders in Liz's class are also saying is that the process of continually asking questions helped them: "I kept asking questions and then deep ones came to mind." This is exactly what happens when adults spend time observing, thinking, and asking questions in small groups. First, they make several observations about an artifact from Central America—a pot with geometric designs on it—then as they listen to each other they notice other aspects and generate other questions. Here is one area where cooperative learning certainly pays off. And we know from research that "organizing students in cooperative learning groups has a powerful effect on learning, regardless of whether groups compete with one another" (Marzano, Pickering, & Pollock, 2001, p. 87).

What we also see here is that questioning improves as we "learn more." The more information we gather, and the more opportunities we have to ask questions about new learning, the better our questions can become. This is most important. We cannot assume that just because students are gathering in more information that they will automatically be curious about it. We must afford them opportunities daily to share their wonderings about what they are learning and have been thinking about.

"Finding out something interesting and finding out why something is the way it is." I like this response because the student is speaking about looking for causes, a very significant critical thinking process. He may be referring to the graphic organizer of questions found in Chapter 6. If you recall the nine o'clock position on this graphic identifies causation as a good dimension to inquire about, especially when we are observing and thinking about human situations as well as about phenomena in nature such as the disappearance of the bees.

What none of Liz's students refer to is the fact that Liz spent a good deal of time helping them become more aware of the kinds of questions they ask. They noted the differences between "Is this Rome?" and other more complex questions such as, "How are religions similar and different?" The graphic organizer of questions was a helpful resource here.

Liz also took some of her students' initial conclusions about religions and helped them go "deeper" by suggesting stems that related the content to themselves, to others, and to religions in general. Students got better because Liz refused to accept their initial conclusions as final. She helped them go deeper thereby providing them with good opportunities to stretch their thinking beyond the immediate, concrete, and most obvious. To do this, Liz had to spend time modeling for her students how we go about drawing conclusions from a comparison/contrast, from a Venn diagram.

We are not finished with this process until we've drawn a conclusion about our comparisons of religions, cars, personal relationships, or works of art.

TEACHERS' REFLECTIONS ON WONDER, INQUIRY, AND INVESTIGATION

One final question I have had about this journey: How has it affected those of us who foster curiosity within our classrooms and for ourselves? It is important to reflect on a daily or weekly basis on what we are doing, how we have worked toward our successes, how we have stumbled, and how well we have picked ourselves up, dusted ourselves off, and started over again to paraphrase a song lyric in the movie "Swing Time" (1936), which Fred Astaire and Ginger Rogers sang and danced to.

Here's a reflection from Kerry Faber, fourth-grade teacher:

I have found that the more I become involved, the more heightened my awareness is of how much I learn by asking questions and seeking answers to the . . . I also find that I, myself, am much more excited about learning. I don't have to plan and direct everything for the children because they have a responsibility for some of what we will learn and the path we will follow in the process. The students, in turn, are more enthusiastic—it's infectious.

> "I have found that the more I become involved, the more heightened my awareness is of how much I learn by asking questions and seeking answers to them . . . I also find that I, myself, am much more excited about learning."
>
> —Kerry Faber,
> fourth-grade teacher,
> Edmonton, AB

Kelly Guzman, a second-grade teacher noted:

I love inquiry-based teaching. I feel that it makes teaching fun! The students are engaged and excited about learning. Even though we do guided inquiry, I still feel that our learning knows no bounds. I always learn new things when I am teaching. I also feel that when I teach through inquiry I am not only teaching students the various content area information—but am teaching them how to be lifelong learners who are independent, empowered, and confident.

When Kerry asked her students why they enjoyed asking questions in class, they had lots of ideas, which are summarized as follows:

The learning isn't boring.

They said they're going home and talking to parents more about what's happening in class.

They are asking more questions.

They want to make "stuff" and bring it in to share.

They are making connections to things they have learned in the past and using that knowledge to continue learning.

Inquiry makes them wonder what they're going to do next.

Here's what Kelly's second graders thought:

Asking questions gets your mind going.

Asking questions makes you more knowledgeable. It helps you set goals.

It is fun to ask and answer.

What comes through in all of these comments is love of learning, the joy of taking some measure of control over your own learning. Kelly speaks of "guided inquiry," where teachers exercise more decision making, but there is still a sharing of intentions and outcomes once we invite students' questions.

There's also the realization from students that questioning helps the learning process. This reminds me of the kindergartner in Della's class (Chapter 1) who, when I asked, "Why do you think it's important to ask questions in class?" responded, "Questioning is part of learning."

Notice also the reference to "making connections." This is Kerry's summary, but I imagine what has occurred within her social studies and science units is that her students, given more responsibilities to ask and answer some questions, are relating what they're learning to previous ideas and topics. This is because our minds naturally seek out connections and, when given time, opportunity, encouragement, and support, students will spend more time relating what they're studying now with what's gone before. That's one of our challenges—to afford students the experiences of responding to questions like these, "How can you connect/relate what we're talking about with what we've studied so far? To what occurs in your own lives?"

Three of Anna Hodge's students (Rock-Hill, South Carolina) shared their reflections on the meaning of inquiry:

Inquiry is the asking of questions to get to a decision or point. For example: If you want to know the answer to something, you ask questions to get to a point and you keep asking. Inquiry can give you reasonable answers. If used, it can guide your every step in life. (Katrice, Grade 4)

Inquiry affects you by letting you be able to learn for yourself and from others throughout your lifespan. (Bobbie, Grade 5)

Inquiry is how people look up answers to a problem that is not able to be stated simply. Inquiry is a way to solve problems. It is a series of steps that reach to the answer. The steps bring you slowly through researching, compiling all of your data and coming up with the final answer. It will guide you through life which creates more connections and more questions. (Logan, Grade 5)

> "Inquiry is how people look up answers to a problem that is not able to be stated simply."
>
> *Logan, Grade 5,*
> *Rock Hill, SC*

What I like about these comments is their focus on asking questions to figure out or solve complex problems; the need for persistence in this effort; how questions beget more questions and help you find and create connections among ideas and that this is a lifelong process: "throughout your lifespan."

I'm wondering if these students have seen the long-term benefits of inquiry on their own or if they'd been taught this directly. I would wager that by fourth grade, if they've participated in an inquiry-oriented curriculum since kindergarten, that they have figured this out for themselves.

FINAL COMMENTS

Planetary scientist Carolyn Porco (2006) has made an observation that seems most appropriate here:

> At the heart of every scientific inquiry is a deep spiritual quest— to grasp, to know, to feel connected through an understanding of the secrets of the natural world, to have a sense of one's part in the greater whole.

All of the wonderings of young students reported here are the beginning of long, long journeys of wonder, inquiry, and discovery. And one of the benefits of these journeys of inquiry is that we become far more connected to the people who surround us, to those who have come before us, and to the world in which we live.

Inquiry leads to specific discoveries, but it also leads to understanding who we are, where we are in the world, and where we might want to go.

Inquiry fosters the "possibilizing" of our lives.

Some of these children may grow up to be the concert pianists, athletes, scholars, doctors, and teachers I heard about one day in the gym at Elizabeth Hall International Elementary School in Minneapolis while working on their goals. If their teachers, parents, and school administrators continue to foster their inquisitiveness, they can become planetary scientists like Carolyn Porco who is now senior research scientist at the Space Science Institute in Boulder, Colorado.

However, it will take more than adult support. Becoming who you want to be will require that they respond positively to what Kerry Faber challenges her special needs students to do every day—take responsibility for their own learning. They must become involved in the decision-making processes that will structure not only their academic but also their personal and future professional lives.

Thus, Howard's question, "Why are mountains necessary?" may launch him toward a career as an earthbound or planetary geologist. And Angelica's question, "How did life begin for fish?" may set her on a pathway toward becoming a marine biologist or a poet. Whatever their goals may be, their lives and those of all their classmates will be enriched by what their teachers and their parents are doing to foster, enhance, and develop their inquisitive minds and spirits. And may they all grow up to be like the great Ulysses who, upon setting forth on his journey of wonder and discovery, beckoned his companions,

> Come, my friends,
> 'Tis not too late to seek a newer world.
> Push off, and sitting well in order smite
> The sounding furrows; for my purpose holds
> To sail beyond the sunset, and the baths
> Of all the western stars, until I die . . .
> To strive, to seek, to find, and not to yield. (Tennyson, 1842)

Our ships await us—we will set the sails, take hold of the wheel, set our course for magnificent destinations, and enrich our lives with amazing and fascinating marvels of wonder and discovery.

Welcome.

References

Algozzine, R. & Ysseldyke, J. (2006). *Teaching students with special needs—A practical guide for every teacher.* Thousand Oaks, CA: Corwin Press.

Amaral, O. M., Garrison, L., & Klentschy, M. (2002). Helping English learners increase achievement through inquiry-based science instruction. *Bilingual Research Journal 26*(2), 213–239.

Barell, J. (1988). *Opening the American mind—Reflections upon teaching thinking in higher education.* Upper Montclair, NJ: Montclair State College.

Barell, J. (1995). *Teaching for thoughtfulness—Classroom strategies to enhance intellectual development (2nd ed).* New York: Longman.

Barell, J. (2003). *Developing more curious minds.* Alexandria, VA: Association for Supervision and Curriculum Development.

Barell, J. (2007a). *Problem-based learning—An inquiry approach.* Thousand Oaks, CA: Corwin Press.

Barell, J. (2007b). *Quest for Antarctica—A journey of wonder and discovery.* iUniverse.

Barell, J. (2007c). *Surviving Erebus—An Antarctic adventure.* New York: Royal Fireworks Press.

Bourgeois, P. (1986). *Franklin in the dark.* New York: Scholastic.

Bransford, J., Brown, A., & Cocking, R. (Eds). (2000). *How people learn—Brain, mind, experience, and school.* Washington, DC: National Academy Press.

Campbell, S. (2007, January). Nathan's Pet Snails. *Highlights for Children, 62*(1), 12–13.

Canfield, J. (2005). *The success principles—How to get from where you are to where you want to be.* New York: Collins.

Copple, C. Sigel, I., & Saunders, R. (1984). *Educating the young thinker: Classroom strategies for cognitive growth.* Hillsdale, NJ: Lawrence Erlbaum Associates.

Cowcher, H. (1990). *Antarctica.* Boston: Houghton Mifflin.

Crane, S. (1955). *Stephen Crane—Stories and tales* (R. W. Stallman, Ed). New York: Vintage Books.

Dewey, J. (1910). *How we think.* Boston: DC Heath.

Ellis, E. (1993, June/July). Integrative strategy instruction: A potential model for teaching content area subjects to adolescents with learning disabilities. *Journal of Learning Disabilities, 26*(6), 358–382.

Fullan, M. (1993). *Leading in a culture of change.* San Francisco: Jossey-Bass.

Ghiselin, B. (1955). *The creative process.* New York: New American Library.

Gleick, J. (1992). *Genius—The life and science of Richard Feynman.* New York: Pantheon Books.

Heath, C., & Heath D. (2007). *Made to stick—Why some ideas survive and others die.* New York: Random House.

Hill, J. D., & Flynn, K. M. (2006). *Classroom instruction that works with English language learners.* Alexandria, VA: Association for Supervision and Curriculum Development.

Johnson, R. (1975). Meaning in complex learning. *Review of Educational Research, 45,* 425–460.

Kashdan, T., Rose, P., & Fincham, F. D. (2004). Curiosity and exploration—Facilitating positive subjective experiences and personal growth opportunities. *Journal of Personality Assessment, 82*(3), 291–305.

Kohl, H. (1988/1968). *36 children.* New York: Plume. (Original work published in 1968).

Kreitner, R., & Kinicki, A. (2001). *Organizational behavior* (5th ed). New York: Irwin.

Lambert, C. (2007, January/February). The science of happiness. *Harvard Magazine, 109*(3), 26–30, 94.

Langer, E. J. (1989). *Mindfulness.* Reading, MA: Addison-Wesley.

Levine, J. (2007). The unorthodox behaviorist. *TC Today—The Magazine of Teachers College, Columbia University, 31,* 2.

Lindfors, J. W. (1999). *Children's inquiry—Using language to make sense of the world.* New York: Teachers College Press.

Lipman, M. (1988) Critical thinking: What it can be. *Cogitare, 2*(4), 1–2.

Lipman, M. (1990). *Harry Stottlemeier's discovery.* Upper Montclair, NJ: Institute for the Advancement of Philosophy for Children.

Marzano, R. (2003). *What works in schools—Translating research into action.* Alexandria, VA: Association for Supervision and Curriculum Development.

Marzano, R., Pickering, D., & Pollock, J. (2001). *Classroom instruction that works—Research-based strategies for increasing student achievement.* Alexandria, VA: Association for Supervision and Curriculum Development.

Marzano, R., Waters, T., & McNulty B. (2005). *School leadership that works—From research to results.* Alexandria, VA: Association for Supervision and Curriculum Development.

Mayer, R. (1989). Models for understanding. *Review of Educational Research, 59*(1), 43–64.

McCombs, B. (1991, April). *Metacognition and motivation for higher level thinking.* Paper presented at the annual meeting of the American Educational Research Association, Chicago.

McPeck, J. (1981). *Critical thinking and education.* Oxford, England: Martin Robinson.

The National Research Council. (2000). *Inquiry and the national science education standards—A guide for teaching and learning* (pp. 125–126). Washington, DC: National Academy Press.

Novak, J. D. (1998). *Learning, creating and using knowledge—Concept maps as facilitative tools in schools and corporations.* Mahwah, NJ: L. Erlbaum Associates.

Parker, J. (1969) *Process as content.* New York: Rand McNally.

Porco, C. (2006). *What is your dangerous idea?* Retrieved January 1, 2007, from www.edge.org

Redfield, D. L., & Rousseau, E. W. (1981). A meta-analysis of experimental research on teacher questioning behavior. *Review of Educational Research, 51(2),* 237–245.

Schibsted, E. (2005, October). Way beyond fuddy-duddy—Good things happen when the library is the place kids want to be. *Edutopia, 1, 7.*

Sheff, D. (1988, January 19). Letters to the editor. *The New York Times,* p. A26.

Shelly, P. B. (1821). *A defense of poetry.* Retrieved March, 2007, from http://www.bartleby.com/27/23.html

Showers, J., & Joyce, B. (1996). *The evolution of peer coaching. Educational Leadership, 53(6),* 12–16.

Sigel, I. (with Copple, C., & Saunders, R.). (1984). *Educating the young thinker—Classroom strategies For cognitive growth.* Hillsdale, NJ: Lawrence Earlbaum Associates.

Sullo, B. (2007). *Activating the desire to learn.* Alexandria, VA: Association for Supervision and Curriculum Development.

Sutton-Smith, B. (1998). *The ambiguity of play.* Cambridge, MA: Harvard University Press.

Ward. P., & Brownlee, D. (2000). *Rare earth—Why complex life is uncommon in the universe.* New York: Copernicus.

Welch, J. (with Byrne, J. A.). (2001). *Jack—Straight from the gut.* New York: Warner Books.

Whitin, P., & Whitin, D. (1997). *Inquiry at the window—Pursuing the wonders of learners.* Portsmouth, NH: Heinemann.

Wiggins, G. (1998). *Educative assessment: Designing assessments to inform and improve student performance.* San Francisco: Jossey-Bass.

Ysseldyke, J., & Algozzine, B. (2006). *Teaching students with learning disabilities—A practical guide for teachers.* Thousand Oaks, CA: Corwin Press.

Index

CORWIN PRESS

The Corwin Press logo—a raven striding across an open book—represents the union of courage and learning. Corwin Press is committed to improving education for all learners by publishing books and other professional development resources for those serving the field of PreK–12 education. By providing practical, hands-on materials, Corwin Press continues to carry out the promise of its motto: **"Helping Educators Do Their Work Better."**